Sunday Suppers and Saltwater Swims

INDIGO RIVER
PUBLISHING

Sunday Suppers
and
Saltwater Swims

Uncover Your Purpose and
Create The Life You Always Wanted

COURTNEY MARTIN

Sunday Suppers And Saltwater Swim: Uncover Your Purpose and Create The Life You Always Wanted

Library of Congress Control Number: 2025919620
ISBN: 978-1-964686-79-0 (paperback) 978-1-964686-80-6 (ebook)

Editors: Jennifer Casey, Anne McDonald
Cover and Interior Design: Emma Elzinga

The cover art and illustrations were created by Pensacola based artist, Kelly Whibbs.

Printed in the United States of America

First Edition

3 West Garden Street, Ste. 718

Pensacola, FL 32502

www.indigoriverpublishing.com

Ordering Information:

Quantity sales: Special discounts are available on quantity purchases by corporations, associations, and others. For details, contact the publisher at the address above.

Orders by US trade bookstores and wholesalers: Please contact the publisher at the address above.

With Indigo River Publishing, you can always expect great books, strong voices, and meaningful messages. Most importantly, you'll always find . . . *words worth reading.*

To Mom and Dad, thank you for teaching me what is truly important in life and for your never ceasing, unconditional love.

To Jared, you believe in me when I don't.
Thank you for loving me through all of it.

To Amelia Kate and Harry, I adore you more
than you will ever know. Thank you for letting me live
this incredible life as your mom.

And to Meme, who showed me how to have courage.
I miss you every day.

Contents

Preface

THE PURPOSE OF LIFE IS A LIFE OF PURPOSE. - BENJAMIN DISRAELI

I have found one common thread that binds us together. One thing most people want, even though it's hard to attain. Now, you might be thinking of money, power, influence, or fame. Almost everyone wants one or more of those, yes, but the truth is, you can't really achieve *any* of those without first reaching your *highest potential.*

While you may look good on paper, have a high-paying salary, a lovely home, and a family to come home to, chances are you still have that small voice inside saying, "Something's missing. There's more to life."

For me, that voice turned out to be louder and more unrelenting than anticipated. That's where my story begins.

I ignored this voice for most of my life, as many do, because it's a disrupter—it disrupts a seemingly "good" life. Most people do not want to replace the known with the unknown, no matter how stagnant or complacent they admit they are. I am in no way judging a "good" life—I have spent most of my life living the good life, going through the motions as many of us do, while simultaneously battling the feeling of wanting more.

It's funny how even the most mundane memories reappear throughout life, often leaving you questioning, "Why do I remember that?" It happens to me all the time, and there's one that has paid me plenty of visits in the last decade of my life. One that I didn't understand the significance of until I turned 39.

In my second-grade classroom, my teacher asked the students what we wanted to be when we grew up. Do you remember how that felt? I do. My mind was boundless as I pictured myself as a doctor, astronaut, or president. I remember sitting in my blue plastic chair, at my tiny desk filled with books, as well as my Hello Kitty pencil box and my daily journal. Colorful posters and maps, class artwork displays, and themed bulletin boards filled the room. Sitting there, I daydreamed about what amazing title I would hold when I was older, because I knew I'd be just that—*amazing*. The thought that I couldn't do something never entered my mind. In that moment, I never questioned my skill set, intelligence, or competence. My heart raced, and my stomach would be in knots as my building excitement took me to the infinite places I could go. I thought of the world as a place with endless possibilities. I could be absolutely anything, and the only thing impossible about that was picking just one.

Reflecting on where my life has taken me, I now acknowledge this recurring thought serves as far more than just a random childhood jog down memory lane. It wasn't coincidental that I'd take myself back to that second-grade classroom during the pivotal moments, such as graduation, landing a new job, or getting let go from one, but also moments of boredom, asking myself, “Is this what I’m going to do for the rest of my life?”. It was my inner voice, or intuition, trying to be heard while I was too busy trying to fit the three-step mold of life: graduate from college, get a job, and have a family. Life happened, that inner child’s wonderment was buried, but not lost.

I had no idea what I wanted to study in college because I hadn’t yet figured out what I wanted to be. Health and wellness had always interested me, so I first chose a nursing major (before realizing organic chemistry and I were never going to see eye to eye). After a semester, I started back at ground zero, knowing I needed to pick another route—again, with no ambition in any one direction. So, I picked the next best thing: a major that most of my friends had chosen, which was public relations.

I graduated with zero motivation to find a job, but still, I felt a sense of urgency. I saw everyone around me landing jobs, buying their first house or apartment, and enjoying their newfound financial independence. I, on the other hand, was back living with my mom, sitting in my old room, clad with pictures, clothes, and wall décor from my college years, echoing the nostalgic feeling of the four, carefree years I had spent not really paying attention to the definitive timeline in front of me. Why did college have to end? I wasn’t ready to grow up. I scrolled through the internet (before LinkedIn was a thing), wondering whether I should just go backpacking in Europe to ‘find myself’? Isn’t that what people do?

It’s no surprise that I never ended up doing anything with my major, instead choosing a career in pharmaceutical sales. The job paid well. They’d give me a car, a laptop, and an expense account. I did this for a few years until there was a company-wide layoff, when I found myself searching for another job. As I sat down to scour the internet, my mind took me back to that colorful classroom with pretty bulletin boards. I felt comfort as I sat in that memory, becoming that young child full of innocence and big dreams, enveloped in the feelings of youthful energy instead of the anxiety I currently carried as an adult trying to pay bills. I thought, "This is the perfect time to start over. The time when I can pick whatever I want to be."

I wanted more for myself than my previous job.

I have always had an entrepreneurial spirit. My family was full of entrepreneurs, so I grew up watching in awe the generations before me build and grow companies that are still around today. I always felt such pride driving by my family's business, with my last name painted on the big building, each time wanting to create something of my own. At this particular time in my early 20s, I dreamed of owning my own boutique selling clothes, shoes, and accessories. But, as quickly as this dream came to me, it left, as I thought about the pressure a small business owner takes on. The next thing I know, I had applied for a medical device position that I ended up getting, and I remained at the company for almost 12 years.

Some of my most beloved memories come from this period, which helped shape who I am today: becoming a wife and mother as my top two. I endured many career successes that reinforced my confidence in being where I should be in life: sales. I also experienced many heartbreaking failures, resulting in me asking myself: *What am I doing here*? Throughout these years, that all too familiar vision of that little blonde girl in her blue chair would pop into my memory, and for a fleeting moment, I'd catch myself wondering *what if*. What if I could do it all over, would I be here? I never allowed the thought to get much further because I was quickly onto the ones that consumed me: *Do I have childcare for my work trip next week? What am I making for dinner? Did I forget the dry cleaning again?*

I would eventually stop long enough to explore this memory as it related to my life and purpose, but first, I had to go through what, at the time, was an ugly transformation that began about eight years prior.

In 2015, I was simultaneously pregnant with my second child and battling to save an over $1 million hospital account. I sold heart monitors, and the hospital had to decide between me and my competitor, giving us several months to show who was the best vendor. It was an extremely competitive situation that completely dominated my every thought and action. In the case that you have never called on physicians, these people are pretty much impossible to catch. This meant I worked overtime to see my key customers, often trying to see them in the early mornings before rounds or after 5:30 pm when they were finished with clinic. I traveled countless miles and hours to see important customers just to be told, "I'm sorry, he doesn't have time to see you today. Try again tomorrow." A whole day wasted…I guess I could have made my daughter's Thanksgiving class party after all.

I would frequently hold presentations in front of intimidating teams of the community's most renowned cardiologists, electrophysiologists, and their staff. It would be me, standing in front of the large boardroom, going slide-by-slide through my PowerPoint, pretending not to be shaken by the disinterest that grew apparent with each click of my slideshow. Within a few days and numerous pep talks later, I'd shake the feeling of defeat and get back at it, only to be met with the office chatter regarding how amazing my competitor and her products were.

With each visit to these physicians, I felt more and more like the underdog, and my once compelling selling skills took more of the form of begging. I felt so much pressure to win, as we all do in sales, not just for a decent paycheck but to keep my job. This was my second-largest account. To lose this account would be completely devastating not only to me but also to my region and company. It seemed like the harder I worked, the more the account and my customers slipped away. I worked hard, but not smart. I toiled out of a place of fear, which my customers definitely saw; not just by my nervous energy alone, but by my desperate attempts to steal the competition by begging people to meet me out for drinks or dinner. Yes, treating them to food and wine would make them like me. I thought I was doing all the right things: I spent several days a week working in the hospital, I brought in directors and VPs to show how important the customer was to our team, and I worked hard to deliver unmatched customer service, never leaving a phone call unanswered. All I could think about was winning this big account—losing it was not an option.

The competitive environment grew to be more toxic than professional, as many of them do. My competitor and I were pitted against each other like school rivals on College Game Day. In hindsight, there was space for both of us; collaboration would have benefited the hospital's patients far more than our egotistical war. But as it goes with any war, players don't fight fair.

I remember one day so vividly. I walked into the cardiology office ready to train some nurses on the hookup process for my monitors when the director approached me.

"Good morning! How are you?" I greeted him cheerfully like I always had.

"Your monitors aren't in compliance with the hospital's certification criteria, so you're going to have to take them all off the shelf right now." He didn't share my same cheerful demeanor, and mine became short-lived.

I looked around the room. Every eye was on me, but no one said a word.

Confused, I stared up at the 12 medium-sized boxes towering over me, trying to figure out why they couldn't stay and how I would pile them on one cart.

As he walked past me, he said, "Oh, and you can't set foot back on this hospital campus without proper documentation."

Out of all the rejections I experienced in my career, this was a first.

"My company can provide sufficient data supporting our qualifications to sell heart monitors—I can send you anything you'd like to see, my company wouldn't be able to service any of our customers without being credentialled."

But he kept walking without acknowledgment, so I took my monitors and left. Eight months pregnant, I (more like my belly) pushed a large, bulky cart out to the parking lot. The uneven pavement made it impossible to walk five steps without a box falling. As I finally got to my car, wiping away tears under my sunglasses, I saw him and my competitor leaving for a coffee date.

I knew what was coming: if my monitors weren't on the shelf for patients, then the only choice physicians had was to use my competitor's. And they did. I got home and was completely exhausted, not only physically from pregnancy, but emotionally and mentally depleted from the battleground of a day I had. I came home feeling like a loser, even though I hadn't lost anything yet. It was a feeling of lack, disappointment, and struggle, as well as an aching back. But I had to put my poker face on, knowing I had an endless list of household chores and a precious child to spend time with.

A lot of people needed me outside of work, and that number was only growing. What's funny is that an outsider would have said I had it all together, despite my internal work struggles. I always kept up my house, laundry, and cooked most of the meals each night. The structure of the household didn't suffer, but my ability to remain present and in the moment with my family did. Looking back, I wish I could say the opposite, because I can never get those days back. My little toddler was so full of personality and spunk—watching funny videos, playing dress up, and dancing in the living room with one of her many princess costumes on. The memories often leave me with feelings of nostalgia and regret. *Did I give her enough of my time and attention?*

I went on maternity leave in July of that year, knowing this was my last baby and that I wanted to enjoy every single second of his infancy, but I couldn't put down work. I even felt guilty about extending my maternity leave to 12 weeks. While I was out, I kept answering emails and customer calls because the anxiety of losing business drove me crazy. I remember being in the kitchen, sleep deprived, nursing my baby, and finger painting with my toddler while taking a call with an angry nurse. For the rest of the day, all I thought about was that office leaving me for the competition. I loved being at home, but hated the thought of my competitor being face-to-face with *my* customers when I couldn't do anything about it. To say I wasn't a present mom is an understatement.

When I returned to work, I continued working to save this hospital account, while making sure I didn't neglect my other customers. While still living this nightmare that I wanted to just go away, I was experiencing the mom guilt of leaving my newborn with a sitter and my toddler at daycare. It was a constant internal struggle of, "Am I doing this right?" I didn't feel like I was excelling at any of my roles: employee, mom, wife, friend, or daughter. Was life like this for everyone? It wasn't fair.

A few months later, I learned I had lost the account. This resulted in a combination of embarrassment, relief, and fatigue, and I never bounced back. I was used to being at the top in sales rankings, winning President's Club, and being acknowledged as a leader. Yes, the sharp decrease in my sales ranking and bonuses was difficult, but the hardest part was losing my confidence and self-esteem. I felt so insecure in my role that I began to silently retreat from the girl I knew.

I had always been that starry-eyed rep who viewed this job as an exciting challenge and sold with the utmost confidence and passion. What happened to her? I never managed to recover from that loss and get back to the rep that I once was. I used to be my manager's go-to girl by helping other under-performing reps in our region reach their sales numbers, motivating the team with my inspirational account wins and latest victories over the competition. They regarded me as a company-wide leader. The CEO knew me by name and would personally congratulate me on my accomplishments. After losing the $1 million account, I was looked at differently.

My weekly calls with my manager went from "Great job this month, you've exceeded your goals yet again," to "According to the monthly report, your numbers have taken quite a hit from last quarter. Because of this, you will need to turn in an extra report each week explaining how many customers you saw each day, what you talked about, where you went, how many miles you drove, and how many sales you made until you get your numbers back up. If there's no improvement within a few months, you'll be put on a performance plan."

The hits kept on coming. They had no idea what I had been put through. I had fought like hell to win this account, battled with epic betrayal and heartbreak, but they couldn't see any of that. All they could see was their daily sales report, which had my name highlighted in red. They started questioning everything I did and everywhere I went: my customer interactions, my paid time off, and even my mileage. Every move was analyzed under a microscope. Why were they coming after me? After years of success, I lost one account and became the enemy. Was I going to have to work longer hours to get my numbers back up? Be away from my family even more? That wasn't fair! I was resentful, no longer felt valued, and now lacked motivation for the job I once loved.

At the end of the year, my company merged with none other than my competitor's. Even worse, that rep that I so badly wanted to see lose? Who won the $1 million account? She was promoted to VP of sales in *our* new company, and now I had to see her name in daily emails, hear her voice on conference calls, and see her stand up on stage at sales meetings. Everyone in the company that we now shared had heard about our situation; everyone knew she had won, and I had lost. Because of the merger, we faced a realignment, meaning some of us were moved from our territories. Due to losing this huge account and my numbers showing stronger east of me, I was also realigned to the South Georgia territory, which was five hours away from my home. Why was this happening to me? I felt like damaged goods.

Somehow, my husband and I made it work, but it was hard and I wasn't happy. Over the course of several years, this unhappiness kept building, affecting every facet of my life. Work kept me from my family more, and I struggled each time I got in the car. This direct correlation between leaving to go to work and my building frustration at work developed. My job kept suffering because I grew numb to my customers' needs. Long gone were the days of jumping in my car to visit a customer who had issues with our website when I could email them the troubleshooting PDF. I fell back into doing the bare minimum, which led to even more customer losses. I never won another award or trip or received sales recognition for performance after that.

I became stuck in this vicious cycle of negativity, unhappiness, and unfulfillment with no idea how to stop it. I was trying to fulfill infinite roles at once, which led to an unbalanced life that benefited nobody. At the time, I thought the emptiness I felt was because I was spread too thin, taking on too much. "If I could just stay at home and not work, I'd be happier," I thought. I spent many days just dreaming of a different life, a life of less stress and more leisure, with no bosses or customers. I wanted freedom from it all and thought that by eliminating my job, I'd be able to fulfill the role 100% of 'mom' and 'wife' and be 100% fulfilled. I wouldn't figure it out until later, but I needed fulfillment, purpose, and just *more.*

I probably would have kept on this track of despair if it weren't for my grandmother's passing away in October of 2021. I had never experienced heartbreak of that kind. She had always been a huge part of who I was, where I came from, and who I would become. I had never done life without her and knew there would always be a piece of me missing from that point on. Being with her as she lay in her hospital bed on those final days, I couldn't help but think about the end of my own life. If I were the one in that bed, would I be proud of the life I built, the legacy I would leave? Could I say with 100% certainty that I gave it all I had, ready to leave this Earth with no regrets? My stomach twisted because I knew the answer: no.

After Meme passed away, life looked different, as it does for many after losing a loved one. Life wasn't a guarantee, but death was. My complacent daze needed to stop. I didn't know what my next step would be, but I knew I had to be brave enough to take the first one. When Meme died, I made a promise to her that I would start *living.*

That following summer, I decided to quit my job, stay home with my children, and finally be the stay-at-home mom I'd always dreamed of being. My last day was on a Friday in May, and I remember waking up the following Monday, pinching myself to make sure it wasn't a dream. I didn't have to bear the "working mom" label anymore; I was just a mom. I took my kids to a friend's house for a playdate that day and made the conscious decision not to answer my phone ...I didn't have a manager or customers demanding my attention. I think I let every call that day go to voicemail just because I could.

I felt extremely fortunate to dedicate my all to my children.

When I think of my childhood, I think of summer. I loved living a childlike summer through my children again, getting a taste of that freedom that I so missed. For the first time, I could take them on day trips to water parks without checking my email for a last-minute conference call. I could enjoy a full day at the pool without looking at my phone, making sure I didn't miss a customer call. I could spend a summer fully submersed, enjoying the longest days of the year with the people I love. I was finally able to breathe...and smile.

When the kids went back to school in the fall, life looked like this: cleaning the house, doing laundry, going grocery shopping, picking kids up, dropping kids off, feeding family on repeat. This is what I wanted. This is what it means to be a stay-at-home mom. Where I shared these responsibilities with Jared before, they all now fell on me. How come all the stay-at-home moms I know make it look so fun? What was I missing? I began again to feel that emptiness. I couldn't shake the nagging thought, "Was this it?" Certainly not, right? It was hard to admit, but that familiar feeling was back: I wanted *more*. I tried brushing this thought off, thinking it was nothing more than a fleeting thought, but each day, multiple times a day, it reappeared. What was the "more" I was looking for?

Don't get me wrong; I loved being a mom and a wife, being home when the kids got home, helping them with homework and spelling words, and making dinner each night. That was my new job, and I loved it. But I couldn't help that the other part of me felt empty. I had everything I wanted, so why was there a part of me feeling so unfulfilled?

Thankfully, the unrelenting Instagram ads saved me. I must have been searching down the cyber self-help aisle because Roxie Nafousi's Manifest: Seven Steps to Living Your Best Life found me.[1] And since I was on a quest to figure out how to live the sort of life that would leave me in my hospital bed at the end of it, fully, unequivocally, and undoubtedly certain I had given my all, with not an ounce of regret…I bought it.

It's about finding your purpose while living in a state of abundance and gratitude, and combating fear and limited beliefs that only serve to hold you back from reaching your highest potential. I didn't even know what I wanted to be, but I knew I wanted something more.

I couldn't put it down; this was just what I needed. I needed purpose, I needed fulfillment. I wanted to carry out what I was put on this Earth to do.

---

1 Roxie Nafousi, Manifest (Chronicle Prism, 2022).

It was then that I discovered a pattern in my life: unfulfillment. Most of my life, I had been seeking something. Amid career changes, new homes, marriage, and children, the underlying feeling of wanting 'more' in the pit of my soul had always been there. My once meaningless memory of sitting in my second-grade classroom, dreaming of what I wanted to be, now made so much sense. It had been my inner child, me, whom I ignored as I went through the motions of life. That voice had been trying to tell me all along I wasn't living my truth, but I had to come to that realization on my own after a lot of heartache and disappointment.

I recognized I had been looking in the wrong direction—externally—for fulfillment. In that moment, I realized joy, gratitude, and abundance lie *within* me, and that it was my job to cultivate these, along with many other emotions, to change my reality. What I'd been searching for was there all along; I just needed the tools to uncover it.

I had no idea I had the power to control my mind and use my brain as a tool. I found it absolutely exhilarating that we actually possess the power to change the narrative and create our own destiny. I didn't want to waste any more time.

I found this science of seeking your purpose and reaching goals so transformative. As someone who experienced such an unbelievable renewal, I wanted to tell my story so others could understand their self-worth and truth, helping others live in the fullness of light. It's not difficult, but a lot of people just don't understand the practices. If you're reading this book, chances are you are seeking the same things I did. We all do at some point in our lives.

Even today, I feel like I'm doing life backwards, often thinking, "Why couldn't I have figured all of this out decades ago, when I was first starting life in my early 20s?" I know most of us feel this way. Why else would the self-help industry be on the rise and midlife crises be a household term? Society and biology have a lot to do with this.

Society the Influencer

I remember lying down with my young son one night. As he was about to close his eyes to go to sleep, he said, "Mom!" in a state of panic. "I don't know if I should be a quarterback like Tom Brady in the NFL or a tight end like Travis Kelce." It wasn't a question of whether he was going to play in the NFL. His struggle was over which position.

Children don't think in limiting terms, just like you and I didn't initially. As children, we had vivid imaginations, turning our beds into pirate ships and couch cushions into tree houses. We were princesses and knights, and each scenario had a fairy-tale ending. Once, we all had that unshakeable confidence of becoming a rocket scientist for NASA or a famous ballerina performing on stage at the American Ballet Theatre.

Many of us would do it differently if we had the chance. If we could start our lives all over, they would look vastly different from what they do now, as we do not honor our intrinsic voice. We as a civilization put a lot of weight on job titles, clothing brands, and zip codes, which directly impact our career choices. When we choose our path in life based on monetary reasons, the effect is almost always unfulfillment because we are valuing societal expectations above our higher purpose.

Just like yesterday, I remember sitting at college orientation across the table from a counselor with my mom by my side. Fresh off the stage from receiving my high school diploma, my biggest concerns were whether my high school sweetheart and I would get back together and whether my clothes were cool enough for college. There were people everywhere, more people than I'd ever seen in a single room at once, and it was freezing cold, despite it being midsummer in central Florida.

The counselor looked at me and said, "What major did you choose?" I looked at her with a blank stare that seemed to last well into the awkward silence stage.

I responded, "Major?" Is she kidding?

She took off her glasses, her expression growing more serious. Impatiently, she said, "Yes, you must choose a major so we can enroll you in the appropriate classes this fall."

The hair on my arm stood up, and my heart raced. My eyes grew large as I looked at my mom, sending her a nonverbal cue that I wanted to go home. I knew, though, that it wasn't up to her; it was up to me and only me. In all my childhood dreams of what this moment looked like, I never pictured myself in a panic at a desk, telling a stranger what I wanted to do when I grew up. At that moment, I was about to change the course of my life, and she was holding the stopwatch.

I looked through what seemed like a novel of majors and quickly went to nursing.

Of course, I ended up changing my major after the first semester, because I chose a career out of haste. Reflecting on my college experience, I can compare it to white-water rafting: someone placed me on a raft, sent me down the treacherous river, and somehow, I made it to the bottom. Still, I was confused as to how I got there. Sound familiar? Unfortunately, the rush to select a major and then later to find a job wasn't self-inflicted; it's the way our society works, the way the world works.

Our world has become too rational, too logical, and too rigid. We must get back to where we came from as children, a place where we relied heavily on intuition, passion, and excitement instead of fitting into the proverbial mold of conformity. As a result, you have people, like me, who stop midlife and question it all. Like, we're suddenly waking up after the dust settles from getting married, having babies, and building homes. We ask ourselves questions like, "Why am I here?" and "What is my purpose?" We often question our innate happiness and fulfillment because we didn't consider those before making any of our life decisions. Many of us brush those questions off because they're intrusive and, let's be honest, *scary*. We are scared to really explore why these words follow us, scared of change and the unknown. But do you know what's scarier? Living a life that doesn't fuel you, living your entire life never discovering your self-worth, and never realizing your incredible, unique gifts and strengths. Disruption, after all, is the gateway to inspiration.

Those annoying questions that often arise? Don't ignore them. They're simply your inner self trying to tell you, "It's your time now."

We all have limitless potential; we just must understand how to unleash that by conditioning our brains and exercising them to align with our goals. I've outlined five simple concepts that you can start implementing and living by today. I'll walk you through how to find your purpose, create a powerful vision, overcome the limiting beliefs of fear and doubt, adopt an abundance mindset, and finally, align your behavior to make it all become your reality.

I truly wish I had discovered these years ago—I would have been happier and more successful than I could have ever imagined. But more importantly, I would have lived life with more intention.

I've designed this book to share my personal journey while sharing the applicable practices that helped me find my purpose and cultivate a purposeful career. I also explain the cognitive science behind these mindset practices which propel you toward the life you desire. With this book, I promise you will gain so much more clarity on why you're here, where you're going, and how to get there. You will be equipped with the tools necessary to start your journey to live the gratifying, fulfilled, and amazing life we were all meant to have. At first, it may seem selfish to take time away from something else to work on yourself, but you can't give to anyone in your life if you're not fulfilled. It may seem counter-productive to write down the things you feel gratitude for before making a grocery list or planning for a meeting, but I promise, it will allow you to give back tenfold.

The one thing I ask you to keep in mind is your own discomfort. With growth comes change, and that's not always a feeling we humans adapt well to. I want you to remember that when you experience this, that means you're doing it right. So, acknowledge this discomfort, get comfortable with it, and *keep going.*

The idea for this book originated from a conversation I had with my husband in our kitchen, and now you hold it in your hands. Consider this your instruction manual for assembling the life of your dreams: a five-step algorithm for cultivating not only what you want in this life but *who* you want to be. You're a few pages away from realizing *what* and *who* has been there the whole time. I will simply show you *how* to reveal them.

While reading this book, know that life is happening *for* you, not *to* you. If there are mental barriers holding you back, we will uncover them together, and you will soon move forward in your goal-attaining journey. This book is a love letter from me to you—I'm giving you all my love and support as we go through this crazy life experience together. I hope you feel that love with each turn of the page, and in turn, give some of it to the rest of the world.

CHAPTER 1

Something Bigger

THE INTUITIVE MIND IS A SACRED GIFT, AND THE RATIONAL MIND IS A FAITHFUL SERVANT. WE HAVE CREATED A SOCIETY THAT HONORS THE SERVANT AND HAS FORGOTTEN THE GIFT.

– ALBERT EINSTEIN

About five years ago, I attended yet another national sales meeting in one of those big conference rooms with no windows. My mind wandered as the vice president stood and droned on about the year's goals and initiatives. Instead of paying attention, I dreamed about what else I could be doing. I pictured myself as my own boss, sitting at a large, oval, cherry-wood table with a coffee in hand, addressing my team of people. They took notes, hanging on my every word. I also dreamed of being at home, living the stay-at-home mom life: making breakfast for everyone, packing lunches, and going to Pilates class with the other moms after drop-off.

While attending sales meetings, we frequently stayed at an upscale resort in southern Florida. As I walked to the conference center in the mornings, dressed in my business suit, I'd pass cheerful families dressed in brand-new bathing suits and cover-ups heading for breakfast, excited for a day at the pool. It made me miss my family, and "mom guilt" would follow. Envious, I would have given anything to switch places with them.

During one conference, feeling and looking like a zombie, I sat down to eat lunch with my colleague Jamie. "I think I'm supposed to be doing something else with my life," I said, biting into the banquet-style hotel food.

"Yeah, me too, but you can't find another job that pays what it does and offers the flexibility like sales does," she responded flatly.

Jamie had a point. My children didn't have to attend an 8-5 daycare. I had arranged my work schedule to make the 1:00 pm pickup time, just like the stay-at-home moms. We could afford nice family vacations and enjoy financial stability. My husband and I were able to purchase a lovely house in an expensive part of town, so the kids went to a good public school system. We had a comfortable lifestyle with little stress, and our children lived the good life. I wouldn't be the reason we had to change it all.

I felt stuck.

Could I be the only one who had these thoughts? Did everyone else love the job, the company, this meeting? Everyone seemed happy to be there, as though they belonged. I felt like an impostor. I told myself to keep smiling, engaging, and acting interested. After all, if I didn't speak up enough, I'd stick out in a room full of ambitious people asking questions and contributing to the meeting. I had to keep up the façade of a career-driven corporate saleswoman, hungry to climb the ladder and break through the glass ceiling. If only they knew that woman was screaming to get out.

At the time, my performance stayed mediocre, just enough to stay off the radar. That method of coasting through work, which I had perfected.

At this particular meeting, my company had asked Robert Fogarty, a renowned photojournalist, to come for a couple of days. Fogarty got his start in New Orleans after Hurricane Katrina. For ten years, Robert led "Dear World," which started when he asked New Orleanians why they loved the city. They'd write their reasons on their bodies, and he'd photograph them. Hundreds of thousands of images later, "Dear World" celebrates the power of a personal story and inspires others to do the same.

My company wanted to emulate that idea and cultivate a similar culture of bringing people together, so they invited Fogarty to photograph everyone in the organization. During breakouts, each rep had a chance to write something meaningful on their hands or arms with a tattoo marker—it could be anything from a word or phrase to describe themselves to their beliefs, dreams, or passions. Since I worked for a company selling heart monitors, many of my colleagues wrote phrases that expressed their love of cardiac care, helping patients, and making a difference in someone's life, such as "every beat matters" and "care from the heart." Some wrote inspirational phrases like "dedication" and "passion."

Oh no. Should I stick to the script and write something like "collaboration and execution"?

During this time, I was pregnant with my second child and still new to this working mom thing. Work life grew tougher and darkened my mindset. I had a healthy toddler at home, another child on the way, and a loving husband—what people pray for every day. I should have been grateful for these gifts, but I couldn't see the many blessings right in front of me. I concentrated on what I didn't have so intently that I ignored all the goodness. I didn't know I could *choose.*

The thought of something more out there for me kept plaguing me—like I didn't belong there, at that meeting. An odd feeling crept up: not knowing where I was meant to be, only that it was somewhere else. Years later, I'd recognize that feeling as my inner voice. But at this moment, I only knew it as uncertainty.

I waited until the very last minute, until I heard the bell signaling us to return to the conference center. I grabbed one of the black markers and quickly wrote *There's something bigger* on my arms and smiled for the photographer.

That day ignited the slow-burning fire within me.

I continued to work for seven years after that photo was taken. Seven more years of rushing through the workday to be at home with my children, at the bottom of sales rankings. More mom guilt, more unhappiness, more failure.

I became someone I didn't like. I was constantly stressed out, rushed, and overwhelmed. I just needed to get through each day. After my grandmother's passing, I grew aware of how precious time was and how I was mishandling mine. I wanted to be happy, patient, and less rigid.

Quitting work was the only answer; I knew it was the key to my happiness. I promised my husband I could sacrifice many of the luxuries I enjoyed and immediately put myself on a budget to prove it. The truth is, I didn't care about any of the "stuff" anymore, so I put in my two-week notice. Problem solved.

If only that had been my problem.

I still wanted more.

Everything on paper said I had everything, but my feelings were contradictory. I became what I wanted to be: a stay-at-home mom and a professional girls' lunch companion. I volunteered at the school, cooked homemade dinner each night, and carpooled the kids around town to play dates. I woke up and could choose to do whatever I wanted with my day—a luxury I had always wanted.

Maybe if I submerged myself completely in household chores, I could make the thought go away. When I quit, the maids were the first to go, so I cleaned—a lot. I taught myself how to do things I used to pay people for, like yard work, pressure washing, and painting baseboards.

But I was stagnant. I wanted to move, jump, and have passion and energy, but I felt paralyzed. This feeling didn't sit well with me—I had quit the high-stress job and had the life I had always wanted, and I grew frustrated. So, I kept myself busy with all the duties of a stay-at-home mom. The busier I stayed, the less I ruminated.

Do you know what's funny about feelings? If you ignore them, they'll find a way to keep bothering you. And this feeling grew so heavy with each passing day, it became evident it wouldn't leave me alone. I felt guilty, like somehow this feeling of needing more out of my life took away from my love for my family—if I loved being a wife and mother so much, then why did I feel like I needed more? Who needs more than that? Was I bored? Did I have too much time on my hands?

I've never thought this much about something, and it drove me crazy. All I can compare it to is the honeymoon phase, when the person is all you think about—every second of every day, in everything you do. This is what I was going through, except I didn't get a date out of it. This feeling of wanting purpose showed up in every conversation I had, every meal I cooked, and every spelling word I called out. I couldn't shake it.

One day, at lunch with my dad, in the midst of discussing kids' sports schedules, I blurted out, "I want to start a business."

"Oh yeah? Like what kind?" he asked.

"I have no idea, but I'd really like to work for myself. I think it would be fun and challenging."

"Well, come up with something that people need."

My mind went to something tangible that would make life easier for people. But inventing something that hasn't been thought of before? I can't do that. That's what scientists and geniuses like Bill Gates do.

At night, I'd pray, "God, if I'm supposed to be doing something else, something more in life, please guide me to it."

I prayed for months, but the feeling remained and my purpose still eluded me. I came to the chapter in my new book, *Manifest,* on how to hear your inner voice.[2] It took me a while to accept. I mean, look inward? It sounded cliché, so the credibility escaped me. Also, praying had always been a one-way street for me, so silence seemed anti-productive.

Then, one day, I returned home from school drop-off to find my husband working in his office. The day before, I had done all the laundry, gone grocery shopping, mopped the floors, and cleaned the bathrooms. Dinner was already simmering in the crockpot. I looked around the house and took a deep breath. There it appeared: emptiness.

How would I get to the bottom of this feeling? I talked to God, prayed, and did everything I was supposed to do. Still, I felt nothing. The walls were closing in. I was claustrophobic in my own house. I had to get out.

So, I set out for the woods with Bogey, my loyal Bernadoodle, and for the first time, I didn't talk or pray—I just walked. I blocked

2 Roxie Nafousi, Manifest (Chronicle Prism, 2022).

out every thought to concentrate on hearing this voice everyone spoke about. But, as I walked, I only heard birds and the roots and rocks under my shoes. No voice. With every passing minute, I grew more and more frustrated, almost to the point of being angry. I could've been vacuuming or organizing closets. What was I doing walking around the woods aimlessly?

This went on for about half an hour, and I started to cry. I had never felt such a feeling of nothingness, like a big ball of purposeless matter. I just wanted to know my next steps in life, why I was here, what I was supposed to do, and why this was all so hard. I cried under my hat, feeling defeated, foolish, and heartbroken—a complete and utter letdown.

God had let me down.

As we turned to go back, I stopped at a massive, old tree my kids loved to climb and sat on the bench next to it to compose myself before going home. I didn't understand why I was suffering through such conflict, why had I brought this on myself? Work stress started looking better and better.

As I sat there, tears still welling in my eyes, I felt something. I later understood it to be my inner voice, God, and the Universe delivering the most powerful message: *Your journey is just beginning. It won't be easy. You have a lot of challenges ahead of you, but I will guide you.*

I heard it: the voice I had been searching for, the one I needed to hear!

I had been running toward something for so long, and when God knew I had no more left in me, He met me right there on that bench. It happened so fast, but right then, I knew I had been created for more; I felt justified in my intuition. It felt like the end and the beginning all at the same time.

At this point, I had stopped crying and felt excited, relieved, overwhelmed, and confused all at once. As I got up from the bench to start walking back home, I thought, "What just happened? What journey am I on?"

No one would believe what I just heard.

Although I left with more questions than I came with, I had this strong, innate feeling of serenity. I had hit rock bottom and been reborn. I suddenly knew the answers were there, even if I didn't recognize them. I knew that if I diligently sought my purpose, my team from above would help me. They loved me and were rooting for me. They had just proven that.

I had been praying wrong: I never stopped talking. I would thank Him for my life and blessings, then ask Him to bless and keep watch over my family and loved ones, to keep us safe, healthy, and happy. Then, I'd end the conversation.

Like a prayer dictator with an agenda, I never thought to stop and listen for guidance.

As the weeks passed, I continued with my meditations, or prayers, but I learned to do less talking and more listening. I began thinking about how often I'd pushed aside my inner voice. It's not a coincidence that this feeling of wanting more, being more, didn't go away. I then understood this as not a feeling, but me trying to guide myself. I just had to get to the point of surrender before I could grasp this.

I took my first step: realizing my purpose's presence, just waiting for me to discover it. I'm pretty determined, so I knew I would eventually. But when? And how many steps are there? I shouldn't have quit working.

At least a couple times a week, someone would ask, "How's not working going? You gonna take up tennis or something now?" or "What do you *do* all day?"

I understood why people were shocked. I suddenly threw in the towel after working 16 years to build a career. They were thinking I certainly had a plan, but I didn't. I didn't know how to tell them about my little classified mission to uncover…me.

By early January, I had accumulated several books about manifesting your best life and finding purpose. I would read and reread them, taking notes and highlighting sections that spoke to me, like studying for an exam. I thought if I read enough books on finding purpose, then I'd find mine.

What fascinated me right from the start was the connection to our primal brains, something I knew nothing about. I learned we have three basic human drives: sleep/wake, hunger/thirst, and reproduction, all serving our brain's drive for survival. Below these primal brain functions, we have positive and negative motivators. The positive motivators include success, health, or happiness, while negative motivators include fear, anger, or addiction. These keep us going, preventing us from giving up. Our "why" protects these motivators by disallowing distractions to deter us from our focus, a primal brain trait relating to survival. These motivators propel us, but resilience pulls us back up when we fall or lose our way. By keeping us resilient, a strong "why" keeps us looking at the big picture, not allowing minor setbacks to prevent us from reaching our goals. It signals to our brains not to give up and instead find another way to accomplish whatever we set out to do.

I had made progress, but the fact that I hadn't found *exactly* what I had been created to do about drove me crazy. It consumed my every thought and grew beyond exhausting...again.

The holidays ended. The kids were back in school, and our savings account had been depleted. Getting back to my morning routine and walking Bogey in the woods, I felt extremely heavy that day, grappling with enormous guilt as quitting my job had left us on a major budget. My husband had been doing well in his job, which was one factor that contributed to us being comfortable with me quitting eight months prior. But soon after I quit, his employer restructured his commission plan, and he began earning marginally less than he had historically.

"What have I done to us?" I thought. We had two young children, and life would only get more expensive. Stricken with anxiety, I endured many sleepless nights during which I'd ask God to help us.

I had never been in a situation where I didn't know our future. Yes, I felt positive I had started on the path to finding my 'why', but at what cost to my family? Here I was in the woods looking for an answer to my being when I should be out looking for another job.

Depressed and defeated, I opted for my earbuds that morning. Several podcasts were my go-to for inspiration, like Oprah's "Super Soul" podcast and "Making Space with Hoda Kotb," which I loved to listen to when I needed an extra pep. My favorite guests were the spiritual gurus who spoke about God with such fierce conviction that I'd leave the podcast feeling reborn and at peace. I also loved hearing stories of underdogs who created extraordinary lives for themselves, who started with nothing in their pockets but a dream and unrelenting drive. I'd visualize myself being on one of these podcasts, with no clue as to my message or topic, but with the intent of generating hope and inspiration for my listeners.

On this particular day, I wanted to hear Hoda. So, I turned on her podcast and selected the first episode on the list, Steve Harvey was the guest. Steve had a tough beginning—he flunked out of school, had been fired from several jobs, and became homeless, living in his car for three years. I thought, *Well, okay, I'm not at that point yet*. He was 39 when he accomplished his dream of being on TV, and from there, he grew to be one of the top TV personalities in the world.

"How do you get back up after having a tough time?" Hoda asked.

"If I could tell a younger me one thing, I'd tell myself 'This too shall pass,'" Harvey replied. He explained that while it may seem impossible and last longer than it should, it will disappear, but you must keep the faith.

I took it as a sign from my team: God, the Universe, and my guardian angels. They were coming together to let me know it would be ok and to keep pushing through. I had to go through this challenging period because what was waiting for me on the other side would be so worth it. That didn't mean the challenges ahead would be easy, but my inner voice told me things would turn out. It immediately calmed my fears and worries for the future. We were going to be ok. I heard the phrase, "This too shall pass," three times that day.

The next morning, I received a call from my mom. We checked in with each other almost every morning, but she had unexpected news this time. She sold our family home a few years back and had been saving money to give to my brother and me. She told me she hadn't known why she had saved it, and that the thought had recently dawned on her that we could use it now. I never let her know how much we needed it because I didn't want her to worry, but I accepted it with enormous gratitude. After we hung up, I closed my eyes, took a deep breath, and said, "Thank you, God." That night, I slept the best I had in a long while.

From then on, I decided to take a different approach: to not be so intense about this process and instead approach it with curiosity and playfulness. I realized that finding fulfillment and purpose isn't a linear timeline; there's no endpoint, so I had to figure out how to enjoy the journey.

I like structure and plans. I like the knowing. I want a beginning, middle, and end.

I had been treating my experience like a to-do list, but finding the meaning of life isn't something you accomplish and move on from. It's more like evolving as *you* do so, really never-ending. Once I wrapped my mind around that, the floodgates opened for me. I peeled away the layers of ego, material desires, and self-consciousness, and when I did, I began to see that child, sitting in awe of the world around her. I wondered what she would tell me she wanted me to be. I wanted to make that little second grader proud of who she'd become. I wanted to be something for her.

One day, while on my routine woods walk, I suddenly felt haunted by my struggles as a working mom. I began thinking about how hard life had seemed and how stress at work greatly impacted my ability to parent like I wanted to. I hated that I sabotaged my work to counteract mom guilt. I faulted myself for not having enough patience, flexibility, and mindfulness with my young children, but I knew I was doing the best I could at the time and needed to forgive myself.

Then, a thought arose like a flower after lying dormant from winter: I can forgive myself by helping other working moms or parents avoid making the same mistakes. I know their pain, frustration, and defeats. I wanted to help people in general, at work and at home. I wanted to help make people happy, successful employees and present parents—both losing battles for me.

"How can I help them?" I asked God.

I prayed on this one, asking my inner voice to tell me if this was my intended path. I asked my team to send me signs.

Make Room for Guidance

That night, I had a dream. My aunt and I were inside this big, lovely house, and I followed her through the downstairs. The house appeared as an old southern home, with big columns, one in which I could see my grandparents living. The mint-colored wallpaper in the dining room, polished silver, and the long dining room table reminded me of them. Some people were walking around, but not as many as were outside.

What was outside? Maybe a gathering of some sort. My aunt led me toward the foyer, opened the front door, and I followed behind. As I looked around, I tried to find people I recognized, but they were too far away, so we kept walking towards them. Then, we crossed the breezeway to the yard, and we passed by my grandfather, Randall, and my great-grandfather, Harry—both widely successful entrepreneurs of their time. They each wore suits and nice, shiny shoes. As they walked past, both slowed almost to a stop and nodded courteously like southern gentlemen. Without saying a word, they both looked at me, eyes filled with adoration and respect, like they were passing the entrepreneurial sword to me, saying, "Now, it's your time."

That dream showed me I could be on the brink of something big, something I had always wanted. It symbolized my rite of passage: the two entrepreneurs of my family handed over the title to me with pride as they walked inside, and I walked out into the big world where they had been. My grandfather and great-grandfather were trying to communicate with me and encourage me to keep going.

They were telling me what they knew to be true and what was coming for me as if they knew the future. I began to see and understand that the life I had dreamed of was already there, that my team wanted what's best for me. If I continued the work, they would continue guiding me. I also began to understand that there are no coincidences. Instead, they're called spiritual synchronicities and serve as signs from the divine. It makes it very hard to give up when you know the whole Universe is pulling for you.

I began to understand that we are spiritual beings having an Earthly experience, led and supported by our angels and guides.

Spirit guides—non-physical entities or energies believed to accompany us throughout life—offer guidance, support, and wisdom to help us navigate our journey. Each may serve a specific purpose, aligning with our unique needs at different stages of life. For instance, one guide may help us uncover our life's purpose, while another might offer emotional healing or protection during challenging times. Some stay with us from birth to death, acting as consistent sources of wisdom, while others come and go, assisting with lessons or transitions. These guides communicate through intuition, synchronicities, dreams, or subtle signs, encouraging us to trust our inner compass and grow spiritually.

Whether seen as spiritual allies, archetypal energies, or aspects of our higher self, spirit guides are reminders that we are never alone in our journey. The more I grew in my beliefs and spiritual practices, the more I saw these beautiful synchronicities around me. Whenever I asked for a sign, I received it.

Synchronicity is the experience of meaningful coincidences that defy explanation by ordinary chance. Coined by the psychologist Carl Jung, it describes events connected not through direct cause-and-effect but through their symbolic or emotional resonance. The Universe moves in perfect synchronicity, operating as an interconnected web where every element plays a role in the whole. Events, relationships, and circumstances align with divine timing, harmonizing with a larger cosmic order. For example, you might think about an old friend and then unexpectedly hear from them the same day, or repeatedly encounter a specific symbol or number during a significant period in your life. These moments often feel significant, as if the Universe is aligning to deliver a message or confirm a path. They are seen by many as signs of being in tune with a greater flow or purpose, acting as nudges from the Universe, spirit guides, or one's own subconscious to pay attention, reflect, or act.

When I ask for a sign, I can receive it in various ways, almost always through numbers. I began seeing angel numbers several times a day throughout my spiritual awakening and still do to this day. I routinely see 111, 222, 333, and 444 to the point of insanity. Each number sequence has a specific meaning, so consider your thoughts and actions when you see these. That will help you better understand what the angels are trying to communicate. If you ask your team: God, your spirit guides, angels, or the Universe for a sign, they will give it to you. Speak it out loud or say it in prayer, and they will respond.

When I first started writing this book, as a first-time author, I didn't know who I wanted to reach; I just knew I wanted to tell my story and help others live their purpose, so I began writing. One day, my limiting beliefs got the best of me, and I began to worry about whether anyone would buy it and whether they would like it. I thought the whole idea was silly and threw in the towel. But before I did that, I decided to ask for a sign from my team to show me if I was supposed to write this book. The next day, I recalled that meeting where I had written "there's something bigger" on my arms. I had forgotten when the photo was taken, so I checked the time stamp, which gave me chills.

The date read Feb 9, 2015—a date I would never forget. It had been exactly eight years before I began writing this book. On Feb 9, 2023, I went to Best Buy, bought my laptop, came home, tore it out of the packaging, sat down, and began to write. The blatant sign that I had received shocked me. It overpowered my doubt, and I never questioned it again.

The Universe will also send you signs like animals, people, or dreams. Have you ever had a loved one pass away, and then suddenly, you keep seeing the same animal or insect that you hadn't seen before? I've heard stories of people seeing dragonflies, hummingbirds, and even flowers blooming out of season after the passing of a loved one. These are signs that they are with us.

The same is true with people. Have you ever gone a long time without seeing someone, then you see them several times within a week? Or someone may be on your mind, and you run into them out of the blue? We write these off as "random", but these are signs from above, trying to guide you in the direction you are meant to go. But our dreams are the most familiar place for us to receive guidance. This is because our conscious brains fall into a sleepy slumber, and our subconscious brains take over. When we can put the logical, rational part of our brains away (conscious brain), we allow ourselves to be guided by our intuition, or God, because the veil between the spiritual and physical worlds is thinnest when we sleep. My grandfather and great-grandfather visited me very vividly in my dream that one night; it was a dream that stood out above the rest. Years after I had it, I can still recall every detail.

But our teams can't interfere with free will—instead, we have to ask them for specific things we want or need. At this time, I heard a prayer that resonated with me, which I continue to use to this day whenever I seek an answer or guidance. "Tell me what to do, where to go, what to say, and to whom." After I speak this, I'm always shown a direction. Once, a person's name popped into my head randomly, which prompted me to text her out of the blue, "Hey, can we talk today?" She answered with, "Yes, I was actually just about to call you." We're now business partners and have successfully built a coaching program for entrepreneurs. Guides love helping us. That's their purpose—they're just waiting for us to ask for it.

With all of that said, we all have guides and angels who will reveal themselves to you if you ask them to in one way, shape, or form. I encourage you to open yourself up to the spiritual realm and promise you will begin to see signs of their love, support, and presence. Their entire purpose is to help us figure out *our* purpose while on Earth—that's their job. They coach us to find our passion and execute on it, which is the reason many of us hear (inner voice) and see (synchronicities) hints dropped throughout our lives, nudging us towards this. Our sole job as humans is to live as our authentic selves aligned with our higher selves.

I knew my purpose: to help people. Of course, there would be a lot more soul-searching and unanswered questions, but I knew I'd find them and cultivate what exactly I was here to do. I had the confidence and patience needed to unveil the life I wanted, which meant being an entrepreneur, helping others, and living free from financial stress. All three things were on the other side, just waiting for me to capture them.

Understanding my purpose gave me a sense of clarity and direction, but I also recognized that purpose alone isn't enough—it requires action. The journey toward fulfillment is not just about discovery; it's about taking intentional steps to bring that vision to life. With this realization, I began exploring practical ways to turn my passion into reality, knowing that small, consistent actions would pave the way for meaningful change. That's why I want to share what I've learned with you, so you, too, can embark on your own journey with confidence and purpose.

Find Your Why

Why are you here? What a loaded question, right? I've often wondered why we aren't born knowing our purpose here on Earth; it would sure make this whole thing easier. But that is the purpose—to find our purpose. It's the entire reason we are here, and it's time to find yours.

I want to give you, the reader, some action steps to take so you can immediately start your journey to purpose. I hope these action items help ignite the little spark in you that grew into a perpetual flame for me.

Let's Journal

I incorporate journaling throughout this book because it helps us see patterns, stimulates creativity, and serves as inexpensive therapy. I love looking back at my old journals because they're like my personal records of what I was going through, thinking, and feeling at that moment. When we journal, we are allowing our limbic brains, the part of our brains responsible for feelings and emotions, to take the lead. This intuitive process helps us bring to life what may be buried under years of rational, logical thinking, creating a space for us to build something new.

First, you must know that you are different from anyone else on this planet for a reason. You were created and hand-selected to acquire specific talents and gifts with the objective of using those talents and gifts to help others. These are revealed through your strengths, hobbies, passions, and interests. If money weren't a factor, what would you do? What fuels you with excitement? Even certain memories that you experience routinely could point you in the right direction. Something within the base of those memories may point to your purpose. Think back to a meaningful moment in your life. Think about the elements of the situation that made it meaningful; these elements will likely represent some of your core values. Was it being together with family that you don't see often? Was it traveling and experiencing a new place with loved ones? These are the things that matter to you, on a deep level.

Write down and explore these prompts below, and you will see how far they take you.

- Your passions
- Your strengths
- Your weaknesses
- Your motivators
- Your values
- Your biggest fears
- Your biggest worries
- Your wish for mankind

Make a conscious effort to feel every emotion during this process, as they serve as stepping stones to the next level. Each cry, each fit of anger, each smile will expose a tiny hint in the right direction. Write down what you're feeling; not only is it therapeutic, but it may help you see which emotions are triggered by certain memories, thoughts, and actions. This isn't easy. Many people go through life never finding their purpose because they didn't have the tools to discover it.

You are holding them in your hand. You will get there, but be patient and allow the process to unfold for you.

Let's Meditate

Meditation is another recurring practice throughout this book. I love it for so many reasons, and frankly, I'm embarrassed I haven't been doing it longer.

Let's back up. I've always rolled my eyes when people have said they meditate. Seriously, who has the time for this? Five years ago, if you told me to sit in silence for ten minutes, visualizing what I wanted out of life, I'd have laughed. Forget finding ten unaccounted-for minutes—where would I find the solitude? When I was home, I had a baby and toddler hanging on me while I was trying to get dressed, clean the house, or cook dinner, and when I was working, I was rushing through the day, trying to see as many customers as possible, so I could make it in time for daycare pick up. After the kids went to sleep, all I could physically and mentally do was fall into bed and wonder if my life was ever going to not feel like a tornado. I thought the only people who meditated had to be retired empty nesters.

It really took me some time to get comfortable with the idea of sitting in stillness and blocking out every thought that crept in. I had a laundry list of things to do, and sitting quietly for any amount of time seemed unproductive. Turns out, I totally underestimated the far-reaching and life-changing effects this unassuming practice had. Meditation just means silencing your mind, in whatever space you feel comfortable in, so you can exercise clear, uninterrupted focus on your thoughts and inner voice.

Find a comfortable position where you won't be distracted by your surroundings. If you're sitting in a chair, make sure your feet are planted on the floor and your spine is straight. If you're sitting on the floor cross-legged, be sure your knees are below your hips. Relax your shoulders and arms, placing them on your thighs. Use this time to release all the tension you're holding in your body, consciously working through your neck, shoulders, back, arms, and legs, all the way to your fingers and toes.

Focus on your breath. Feel yourself inhale and then slowly exhale. Envision yourself breathing in all the good energy the world has to offer, while slowly releasing all the negative thoughts you may be holding onto with each exhale. Feel your lungs expand with each breath in and relax with each breath out. Concentrate on this movement until you feel totally relaxed and centered.

Close your eyes and silence your thoughts, worries, and concerns—this is one of the most important steps you will take in your journey to greatness. Each time a thought enters your mind, picture it as someone walking through your door and you shutting it. Once your mind is still, you can continue focusing on your breath, maintaining that state of complete relaxation and rejuvenation, or you can listen to that inner voice. If you're using meditation for inspiration and creativity, then make sure you listen to what that voice is trying to tell you. To do this, you must be completely still physically and mentally. Focus on the things that mean the most to you in this world. If you had the superpower to do anything, be anything you wanted to, what would that be? If you could snap your fingers and make *blank* go away, what would that be? Lean into how you feel when you think about these things. As mentioned before, subtle hints throughout life may direct you, sometimes via memories or recurring feelings. Try to uncover these while meditating.

If you are pressed for time, it's a good idea to set a 10-minute timer. This way, you alleviate yourself of the time burden to be fully present. Some people prefer to practice mindfulness frequently in shorter increments, while others choose less frequent, longer sessions. Decide what works best for you and stick with it—the key here is practice and consistency; the more you do this, the easier it becomes. Eventually, you will crave this time to yourself and make it part of your daily or weekly routine.

If you're like I was and are new to meditation, I recommend searching online for guided meditations. So many websites are dedicated to the practice, and I encourage you to explore them further. One of my favorites is the Insight Timer app. It has many different meditation topics personalized for everyone's needs.

I also want to point out that meditation doesn't have to be still. I consider it meditating when walking either along the sidewalk or in the woods with my pup. Being submersed in nature calms me, taking me out of fight or flight, allowing my parasympathetic nervous system (PNS) to take over and mindfulness to occur. PNS is one of the two main divisions of the autonomic nervous system, which regulates involuntary body functions. Often referred to as the "rest and digest" system, the PNS is responsible for conserving energy, promoting relaxation, and supporting restorative processes in the body. By counterbalancing the "fight or flight" response of the sympathetic nervous system, it slows the heart rate, stimulates digestion, and encourages the repair and maintenance of tissues. Activation of the PNS helps maintain homeostasis and supports a state of calm and relaxation, enabling the body to recover from stress and function optimally. Within this state, we can "hear" that inner voice the clearest, and you activate it simply by deep breathing.

Final Thoughts

As you continue your quest for your purpose, you will automatically build confidence as you begin to see and understand yourself better. This is a sign of self-actualization signaling that you're on the right path, moving closer to living as your true, authentic self—no masks, no more disguises. When we can unveil who we truly are, who we've always been, we stop making excuses and live in our truth.

Following your intuition is the portal to living the life of your dreams. I carried around such a heavy heart for what seemed like eternity because I yearned for something more so badly. God put that burning desire there so I'd be left with no choice but to uncover it. He knew that for me to reach that pinnacle of my highest self, I had first to get to know myself, understand who I was, and understand why I was here.

We are all here for a reason, all of us; there are no mistakes. And all our reasons are connected, which connects every one of us to each other by design. Serving a higher purpose is a gift because everything else seemingly falls into place after that. It is the foundation of the meaning of our existence. Finding our "why" will lead us to find our way.

You know that famous saying by Maya Angelou, "You can't really know where you're going until you know where you have been?" I finally understand the meaning of that statement. We must first look back, observe the patterns, and connect the synchronicities that our life has been comprised of thus far. When we allow ourselves to explore our pasts, we begin to see our most challenging experiences, significant defeats, and painful heartbreaks play a role in our purpose. The most memorable events are little glimmers of our higher selves, subtle hints guiding us to our ultimate potential and purpose. By seeking this, everything else in your life will unfold, in due time, and fall into place.

You've heard the voice but may not have recognized it. You've felt this feeling but may have buried it. You may have seen the signs but ignored them. But now's your time. It's time to hear, feel, and see your 'something bigger'.

CHAPTER 2

Vision

It's not magic; it's just that you are able to see the possibilities to move forward with your dreams in a way that your brain was hiding from you previously.

– Tara Swart, The Source

I am a dreamer who has always had big, big dreams. When I wanted to open a clothing boutique, I didn't just settle for one—I knew I'd have at least three, scattered around several counties of Florida. As a board member serving a women's and children's nonprofit organization, I was privy to the transportation issues affecting a certain demographic in our city. I spent many hours and days researching how to create a free commuter system to transport people to and from doctor appointments. I even contacted a taxicab company (this was before Uber) to inquire about contracting with me. When I was in sales, I wanted to build a database that housed competitive intel so device reps could see where to go for business...and then sell it to a company like Salesforce.

I've always wanted to be extraordinary and change the world. That starts with a dream. Having dreams, big or small, is part of the human experience, and many times, it keeps us going when we have nothing else to hold on to. Dreaming has been my escape when I yearn for a different circumstance. I like to pretend I have a magical button that, when I hit it, instantly transplants me to that place in my dreams—like a time machine, but a dream machine.

I have two favorite dreams. The first is living a life of freedom: travel, financial, and stress. In this dream, I'm usually at my beautiful beach house, watching my children play on the beach while I bask in the feeling of lightness, stripped of life's anxieties and instead living each day with a sense of adventure and abundance. My second dream is a genie granting me three wishes. I love dreaming of a fantastic life, of all the "what ifs", and I will never stop.

But I admit there was a period where I found myself growing tired of dreams, right after my grandmother died. I had become impatient with my dreaming state—how many dreams can one have until they finally realize that dreams don't come true via fairy godmother visits? At that pivotal time, death made me more present than I had ever been before. I realized I didn't want to dream for the rest of my life—I wanted to *live* a dream, to create the life of my dreams, and for the first time, it dawned on me that I could. I knew I had nothing to lose if I went after one of my dreams and fell short, at least I can say I dared to try. And if I didn't? I'd be in the same spot dreaming, but eventually, without time on my side.

Why did it take the loss of my grandmother to figure this out? I first had to let myself (without laughing) believe I was worthy of my dreams. Every inventor, every business owner, every person who creates something first starts with a dream. The only difference between them and I had been self-worth. But why does their worth come with a higher price tag than mine?

We're all humans, got here the same way, and will all exit the same way. What's in the middle is a choice. Whether it was my beloved grandmother's passing or a midlife crisis, something in me wanted to make that choice. I had been living in a one-dimensional black-and-white film that was suddenly upgraded with added dimension and color, and my role was being promoted to lead character. Why wouldn't I go for it? For the first time, I wasn't trying to impress anyone but me. I wasn't trying to fit the mold. I wasn't trying to follow the script. I was *writing my* script. I had an epiphany: no one was going to give me the self-worth I needed to make a shift. No one would make my dreams come true for me—the genie wish never came true. The way I saw it, I could choose for myself or not.

Why was this so hard? Why was I scared? The reason, it turns out, is that we are hardwired to resist change. Our primal brains, or reptilian brains, evolved in the Paleolithic Age, beginning 2.5 million years ago, when we were hunters and gatherers and lived primarily as nomads, escaping brutal climates in search of more humane, livable conditions. Biologists conclude that it was this era when our brains naturally adapted to this time's behavioral and social environments, specifically aiding in survival. Fast forward to today, and we're still operating under these same primal mindsets, and the problem with that is they're not designed to help us navigate our new, modern world.

They often hold us back from reaching our fullest potential because they don't like change; they want comfort and reliability. The strongest driver in our brains was, and still is, survival. Have you ever wondered why changing something about yourself is so hard? Have you ever wanted to take up a new sport, change careers, or reach a weight-loss goal? These all require behavioral changes that will not happen unless you know how to block those primal brain mindsets in the form of fear and doubt. When we step outside of our comfort zones to seek change, our brains will immediately try to hold us back from the unknown because that survival instinct is what kept our ancestors alive. This is the exact reason why many of us, despite our best efforts to grow and change for the better, fail repeatedly because we do not know how to block those limiting intrinsic beliefs.

Once I understood our brains were stuck in the Stone Age, I knew how important it was for me to take ownership and control of my thoughts. Our brains evolved and adapted to our environment so humans could have their basic needs met. Today, our triumphs and struggles differ significantly from the Paleolithic Era, so it's up to us to be conscious of our outdated ways of thinking and work towards manually adapting our brains to modern times.

Realizing this was why I had never acted upon my dreams thus far, I felt this sudden sense of control over my future. I sincerely believed I was worthy and capable of living an exceptional life beyond my wildest dreams, but how do I take action at this point? Where do I even begin turning my dreams into reality?

I took such a fascination with the history and biology of the human brain; I wanted to understand more. I was shocked to learn the magnitude of control we have over our brains and how underutilized this control is. We must tell our brains what and how to think to have desired outcomes. Who knew? Don't they just…know? No, it turns out. You must deliberately and intentionally influence your brain to get what you want. If I can control my brain to get what I want, I'm basically my own genie.

But I needed a lamp to grant myself wishes, and that's where visualization comes in. Visualization is a neurologically proven method that people have been using for centuries to obtain desired outcomes by envisioning exactly what they want on a consistent basis. Doing so, their brain begins to think the visions are reality. From there, you automatically change behaviors and adopt abilities and mindsets that help move you closer to your goal.

I now know why I've always liked dreaming; it's because my brain perceived it as really happening. This is because the human brain cannot differentiate between a vision and reality—the imagery and the reality of that same thing share the same neural circuit, meaning your brain doesn't know the difference. And if your brain doesn't know the difference, we can trick our brains into thinking something—a dream or vision—is actually *happening* to us. That's why I like daydreaming so much—my brain routinely thinks we are on the private island I purchased with the sale of my software company.

Visualization stimulates your brain and promotes the growth of neurons and neural pathways through neuroplasticity, or your brain's ability to change, resulting in a new way of thinking and new behavioral patterns. Learning a new language, how to play a new instrument, or even recalling a memory, we are experiencing neuroplasticity. Until recently, scientists speculated that our brains stopped growing and changing once we reached adulthood; however, with advancements in neuroscience, brain scanning, and research, we now understand the brain's ability to change throughout a person's life.

Powerful examples of neuroplasticity include overcoming addictions and destructive lifestyles, as well as learning how to walk and talk again after brain trauma. Neuroplasticity happens when you're experiencing growth or change, such as getting over a bad breakup, mourning the loss of a loved one, or shifting careers. With each challenge you overcome, you are growing at a cellular level, expanding your brain structurally. When we grow, our brains grow. This rewiring of the brain provides us with a new, innovative way of thinking necessary for our new situation or venture.

Neuroplasticity can happen inadvertently, such as the loss of a loved one, or intentionally, through techniques such as visualization and mindfulness, allowing us to control our thoughts, emotions, and fears actively. This means we can consciously change how our brain thinks to help us seek opportunity, reach goals, and ultimately get what we want out of life. Because of this, we can retrain our brain's primal thought processes to help serve us in our modern lives. This is quite empowering, as is the fact that we have such control over our lives and our destiny. We can make our brains work to create the life we want, to be who we want, and have what we want; we just need to be shown how.

When we have a powerful vision, we are slowly breaking away from the chains of our primal brains and being propelled toward a more success-driven and focused way of thinking. We realize opportunities we hadn't noticed before and take risks we wouldn't have dared to entertain. This is because our brains are task-oriented. For example, you know how you can be in a conversation with someone and forget a name, "it's on the tip of my tongue," you'll say. And it bothers you even after the conversation is finished, and possibly hours or days later, you remember the name. When you give your brain a task, it will search for the answer until it is completed. When we visualize, we're essentially tasking our brains to lead us to a specified goal or outcome. So, by showing our brain via visualizing what we want, where we want to go, and who we want to be, with consistent practice, our brains will lead us there. This means we can turn our visions into reality... or even make a dream come true.

So, that's why I never became an astronaut—my parents left out the part about visualizing when they said I could be whatever I wanted growing up. This was life-changing for me. It meant I had control over my circumstances, future, endeavors, and everything! It felt so incredibly empowering that I could create whatever life I wanted for myself and my family. But again, no one was going to do it for me.

So, I began implementing this practice right away through meditation.

See it to Have It

I remember one day when I was still new to meditation, I struggled with keeping my impostor thoughts away from the grocery run, the items for the class party, and the bills I needed to pay. It was a cold day outside, mid-January, and I was in my room, sitting on the floor with a pink yoga mat under me. As I started to quiet my mind and visualize my future, I hit my first roadblock. I had nothing. I didn't know what I wanted to do, so how could I visualize it? So, I decided to begin with a feeling. I knew I wanted to feel whole, fill the void of wanting more, and feel the most complete when I helped people. I visualized bringing hope to others, helping them out of a hard situation, and improving their lives. I concentrated on how it would feel to open my eyes each morning, knowing I was about to encourage the burnt-out employee, and on the feeling of helping a working mom navigate the stresses that come with balancing it all, helping her prevent going down the path I went down. I felt rejuvenated and alive when I immersed myself in this life ahead of me, the life I was creating. I was getting a taste of what it feels like to live out your purpose, a feeling of true happiness and completeness.

I knew this feeling was telling me I was on the right track. I was learning to trust my intuition and let go of my preconceived ideas of what my life 'should' look like and the timelines that ensued. Visualizing myself helping people from my most vulnerable point made me feel whole, like I had finally found the missing piece. But I was scared to peek over to the other side, nervous about what I might find. I very much enjoy a plan, and this wasn't part of the plan. My whole life plan looked like this: work and make money so you can have financial freedom and little financial stress. I did a job and got paid by my employer—I knew that paycheck was coming every two weeks. I felt safe with that and was able to plan for the future. Now, I had thrown that all away. I had no idea where I was going or what I was doing. There was no definitive. No plan. Super annoying.

But I kept going because I knew if I stopped, I'd end up right back in my dream machine...in the land of black and white. Also, that annoying saying about doing the same thing and expecting a different outcome kept plaguing me. So, I kept visualizing, and soon my visualizations progressed into teaching others through workshops, seminars, and consultations. I saw myself delivering inspiration to a room full of people seeking answers. Where was this coming from? And what would I teach? I pictured the exact room: square with tan walls, carpet (why carpet?), and rows of chairs before me while I led the audience to seek their fulfillment.

I visualized their smiles, words of appreciation, and even hugs of gratitude. I engaged every sense I could to bring this visualization to life because I knew it would lead me there if I showed my brain what my goal looked like. With every visualization, I grew closer to making it real.

One day, my husband came to me regarding issues he and some of his colleagues were having. (Since he works from home often, we regularly meet in the kitchen around lunchtime to discuss upcoming plans, kids' activities, and life in general.) He was standing up, making lunch, and I sat at the kitchen island with my latest manifesting book.

As he sat down at his laptop, sandwich in hand, he said, "Well, it's going to be pretty impossible to hit quota this quarter." Great, financial anxiety just got heavier.

"Why is that?" I asked.

"We are on a nationwide supply shortage, including our lab equipment and supplies, if I can't get my customers these products soon, I'll lose them to the competition."

As he began sharing what weighed on him—supply issues with products, high quotas, and competitors—I noticed the problems weren't due to a lack of skills or talent but were the direct result of the wrong mindset. I've always been so intrigued by how my husband can sell without the customer knowing he's selling. He's one of those salesmen who isn't even pushy, has a conversation with you, and suddenly, you're buying. He's one of those.

Now, had I not been learning about the power of the mind to create our desired futures, I would have consoled him and encouraged him to keep working hard. But I didn't do that; those thoughts never even occurred.

"You have more control than you think, all sales reps do," I said.

"What do you mean?" he asked.

"Right now, you're only thinking about what's not working, not what's well within your control to grow your business. You'll always have hurdles; it's how you choose to handle them and turn them into opportunity."

I began to share with him what I had learned about blocking limiting beliefs, seeking opportunity and abundance, and visualizing success. I explained to him that, despite the situation, we are more in control of our future than we had thought.

Ah-ha!

I knew what I wanted to do in that exact moment: I wanted to help people find happiness, success, and fulfillment by developing the skills I had learned through my journey. I literally went from not knowing where I was going one second to seeing my purpose with crystal clarity the next.

"I figured it out," I said to Jared. "I'm going to help people find success and reach their goals utilizing mindset practices."

My purpose comes from helping people get out of a place where I've been, the place where I felt like no role I filled was good enough. I had to go through what I did—all the stress, worry, sadness, disappointment, embarrassment. It had a purpose. God had me go through and feel all of it so I could use it to help people. It wasn't happening *to* me, it was happening *for* me. Something I absolutely wasn't aware of at the time.

I was experiencing the effects of neuroplasticity. By keeping my vision at the forefront of my mind each day, what I wanted to do became clear to me because I primed my brain to notice opportunities. Using visualization's power, I gave my brain a roadmap to guide me to my goal.

I have a friend, Anna, who went through a life-changing experience that many can relate to. After having her three children in a relatively short time frame, she said she felt a sudden loss of control, like life was happening too fast to keep up with, and she was just a bystander, watching it from afar. Life was happening *to* her instead of *for* her. After having bouts of anxiety, she slowly withdrew herself from the life she once knew and went into a sort of hibernation to pause, reflect, and heal.

One day, she decided to change the narrative and began visualization. Anna told me that she didn't just visualize her future family or occupation, but her entire life. She visualized her future house and what it looked like. She envisioned who was there and what they talked about. She accounted for each second of the day and pictured what she wanted that to look like, encompassing every interaction and the feelings associated with each. She visualized her three children going to school, having play dates, and attending sporting events. She looked deep into the future, visualizing her children grown up—what did their children look like? Where did they live? She wanted to be clear on what she wanted her future to look like, even down to the legacy she was leaving behind.

These powerful visualizations gave way to a life she would never have known was possible. Through her inner work, she came out of her darkness with so much clarity and strength. She started living with intention, working on her hobbies, and cultivating her talents. By visualizing every aspect of her life, she provided herself with a personal roadmap, highlighting where she wanted to go from start to finish. Today, she is a successful business owner and well-respected entrepreneur.

This story was so compelling because, like me, Anna wanted to change the direction of her life. It took her a difficult period to finally decide she was going to write the rest of her story, and visualization revealed to her what her story looked like. Once your 'story' treks from your thoughts to your vision, it becomes your future if you allow it to.

A huge component of successful visualization is always focusing on your goal. Author and radio personality Earl Nightingale once said, "You become what you think about most of the time."[3] This means you must be conscious of every thought and be intentional when selecting your thoughts.

The RAS, or reticular activating system, helps you do just this. It sits at the base of your brain, where it connects to the spinal cord. Its function is helping us focus; Ruben Gonzalez, author of *The Courage to Succeed*, explains that the RAS is like a filtering system, sorting through the eight million pieces of information that flow through the subconscious part of the brain daily.[4] Without it, we wouldn't be able to function—millions of stimuli continually bombard us, and without the RAS, we wouldn't be able to focus on a single thing at any given time. The RAS allows only the messages that are important to us to be passed from the subconscious to the conscious part of our brains, eliminating the unimportant "stuff."

---

3 Earl Nightingale, The Strangest Secret (Nightingale-Conant, 1956).

4 Ruben Gonzalez, The Courage to Succeed (Aspen Press, 2004).

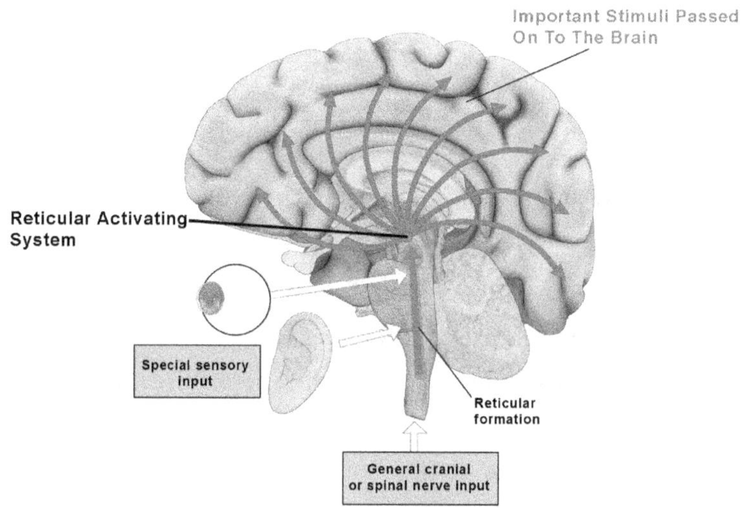

Have you ever been in the market for a new red car, and then suddenly, everywhere you turn, you see a red car? This is the RAS at work. This is why goal setting is so important, and why keeping these goals in your mind is equally important. When you tell your brain what is necessary, the RAS will ensure you only receive the messages supporting that goal, helping you bring those dreams and goals to fruition.

Think of visualization as getting you and your brain on the same page, so the two of you align. You want your brain working with you when it comes to attaining a specific goal, and this is a proven way to accomplish that. When you start this practice, remember it's the end game that matters, with the most important question being, "How do I want to feel?" I did not have a defined goal when I began, but because I concentrated over and over on how I wanted to feel each day, it took on a more distinct direction. My visualizations kept building upon helping people in general, helping parents, and working with parents in sales, ultimately leading me to a particular niche: creating an online course for corporate sales organizations.

Uncover Your Vision

The more you practice techniques like visualization and meditation, the more seamlessly ideas will flow to you, and you will be able to solve problems with greater clarity and ease.

I want you to think of this as a journey, and your 'why' is the key that starts your engine. Visualization is your roadmap. From here, you will experience unknowns and detours along the way, but I will show you how to overcome these hurdles and come out stronger and more resilient on the other side. Enjoy your quest to greatness, and remember: our mind doesn't know the difference between powerful visualizations and reality, so why not put down everything you have dreamed of acquiring or accomplishing? Don't let fear or limiting beliefs hold you back; this is your new, improved future self, just waiting to be discovered. There are a few visualization techniques that will help you get started. My advice is to be consistent; try to carve out at least ten minutes each day, morning or night, to listen to that inner voice. This is your time to reflect, grow, solve problems, and show gratitude. Give it a try, and I promise you'll be hooked.

Let's Journal

Write down each category and explain how your future self looks and feels for each one. What does your day look like, beginning when you wake up? Who do you see? Visualize what you wear when you're at work or home, and what car you drive. Where do you vacation? Each detail will bring you closer to your goal. Just by writing down your thoughts and feelings, you can begin to see a pattern of what influences your mood and impacts your emotions. This will help you associate the different people and situations you come across each day with positive and negative feelings, and it will help clarify your vision of who you want to be, what you want to do, and where you want to go.

Decide on your timeline. I started by asking myself where I wanted to be five to ten years from now; this helped me form a shorter-term plan and set my goals accordingly. Thinking long-term may be too overwhelming for some people, so feel free to break yours down to a period you're comfortable with. You can choose to do a six-month, one-year, five-year, or all three timelines.

You can journal with a pen and notebook, your computer, or a journaling app, but any way you choose, make sure it's easy to use so that you use it regularly. How you want to organize your visualization journal is like this:

- Your goal (if applicable).
- Daily communication: Who do you interact with? How do others react to you? What's their body language, attitude?
- What do your surroundings look like? Where do you go to have the most significant impact? What does that look like? Picture yourself in the exact place.
- What actions will you take each day to reach your goal?
- What inspiring thoughts do you have around this goal?
- How does it feel when you reach it? Where are you? What do you do? Who do you tell?

Write down all your emotions associated with the feeling of succeeding. Try to journal consistently. Write about your goals, thoughts, emotions, plans, and anything else. To help you think of journaling topics, you can also use journaling prompts like:

- What action can I take today to make progress toward my goals?
- What tasks have I accomplished so far to work toward my goals?
- Is there anything holding me back from pursuing my goals?
- What emotions do I feel when I think about my goals?
- What does a dream day in my life look like?

A vision board is an excellent option if you are a visual person. Just like you are your own life's creator, you are your board's creator. Use images from magazines or the internet to depict what you want your life to look like. Use your favorite colors, write your favorite quotes, and cut out pictures of people who inspire you. If success looks like a fancy sports car, put that exact car on your board. If happiness to you is finding your soul mate, choose pictures depicting those feelings of warmth and love. What does your ultimate fulfillment look like? It can be as elaborate as you want it; just make sure it makes you feel excitement—and possibly a spark of motivation—when you look at it.

When I first heard about vision boards, the first thing that came to mind was a collage I had just helped my daughter do for school, filled with her interests, hobbies, family details, and so on. Again, I thought, *Do I have time for this?* But it was part of the seven steps to manifesting, as in Roxie Nafousi's book, so I tried it.

I split my dream board up into specific categories:

- Personal growth
- Love/relationships
- Friends/family

- Career
- Hobbies

Then closed my eyes, sat in stillness, and visualized what I wanted each of these to look and feel like. I was as detailed as possible, uncovering every little aspect of my new life. I printed pictures off the internet, cut some out of magazines, and wrote inspirational quotes. I created my board in a particular way so that whenever I looked at it, I would immediately feel a sense of happiness, a knowing that I could have everything I desired. Whenever I needed an extra push during the many lulls along my journey, I'd bring it out to rejuvenate my passion and excitement for future successes.

Let's Meditate

Visualization meditation is one powerful way to connect with your purpose and gain clarity on your path. This practice lets you quiet your mind, tap into your inner wisdom, and vividly imagine your desired life. By engaging your senses and emotions, you can create a mental picture of your goals as if they have already been achieved, reinforcing your belief in what's possible. Visualization meditations help you stay motivated and align your thoughts and actions with your dreams. As you close your eyes and immerse yourself in this practice, you'll begin to see the steps unfold before you, guiding you toward the life you're meant to live.

Get into your favorite "meditation" position: sitting, lying, or walking in nature. Remember to silence your mind by focusing on breathing to activate the PNS (the calm, relaxed system) and get into your zen zone. I want you to really practice being completely present, not dreading the duties of tomorrow or spiraling over yesterday's mistakes. The present is a gift to you; use it thoughtfully.

Be crystal clear on what you want and how you want your future self to look. Even if you don't know precisely what that is, how do you want to *feel*? Happier? More fulfilled? At peace? What would excite you if money, love, and success weren't issues? Be unapologetic about what you want. Visualize these feelings consistently, and they will ultimately lead you to a more defined goal.

Try to be as specific as possible, including all five senses. For example, if you want to purchase or build a new home, let your mind take you to that house. What color are the shutters? What do you see when you walk through the front door? Do you smell fresh paint? How do you feel in that moment? All these details are essential for a successful visualization—you have to tell your brain exactly what you want and what it looks like so it can lead you to the opportunities to get you there.

If you find a monetary goal difficult to connect with, it's important to lead with your "why." As discussed in the first chapter, a strong "why" is a primal brain function designed to help keep us from distractions and strengthen our focus. This dollar amount must mean something on a deep level for you to manifest it. This will create a personal connection with that number, which will help you persevere during the challenging times, enabling you to see the big picture. So, ask yourself "why"—will this amount of money help put a down payment on your dream house, for example? Will it go to your child's college fund?

Spend time thinking about how you want to feel for each one. How does "new you" conduct yourself day to day? What are your habits? What are your values? Who do you choose to surround yourself with? What do those relationships look like? You are destined to unleash the most empowered, authentic version of yourself, so don't hold back and dream big.

I thought about what living as my higher self in my dream life would look like. How would I feel each morning when I woke up? What would I see? How would my relationships look, and which relationships would I keep around?

I sought utter fulfillment; I wanted to feel like I was fulfilling my life's purpose by helping people every day. I saw myself financially independent, giving my children the gift of travel, and even living in my dream home. I envisioned that every relationship I chose to surround myself with would be meaningful and include encouragement, support, and nourishment. In my marriage, I saw unconditional love and gratitude. As a mother, I saw patience, engagement, and presence.

Submerge yourself in your vision, making it as real as possible, and trust that it's already becoming a reality.

Final Thoughts

Finding your purpose is about figuring out the person you want to become. Picture this: what would your life look like if you could do it all over again? What would you change? What would your dream life look like if you could have it all (and you most certainly can)? This is the new, elevated you—who do you want to be?

This is your chance to dream like you did as a child, unbridled and free. Give yourself permission to think big and put all your energy and power into that goal so that your brain will help you attract new insights, opportunities and welcome new experiences—all of which will help you fulfill your goals and have the life you want.

CHAPTER 3

Beliefs

WHETHER YOU THINK YOU CAN OR YOU THINK YOU CAN'T—YOU'RE RIGHT. – HENRY FORD

Limiting beliefs are perhaps the planet's most potent, powerful, and dominant yet intangible objects. And I use the word 'objects' loosely. We can't touch them; they don't have a physical nature, but their mere presence cannot be matched. We allow them to make countless decisions, and the more important the decision is, the more we lean on them to decide for us. We listen to these thoughts of doubt as if they know what's best for us, like they're protecting us from making huge mistakes and failing. We hold so much regard for these beliefs that we are tricked into thinking they're our reality, never questioning their motives or objectives. The actual reality is that these invisible impostors stand in the way of our hopes, dreams, goals, desires, and highest potential.

Hi, my name is Courtney, and I'm a prisoner of my own thoughts.

When I was young, I always heard, "You have really pretty blue eyes," or "Wow, you're a really fast runner." These are both very nice compliments, but I yearned to hear, " You are so smart."

I was 9 years old and had this friend Megan whose family was big college football fans, and they'd frequently invite me to stay with them in their motorhome for a game weekend. I was always so thrilled to be able to join them on these trips, and riding in their nice motorhome was such a treat for me. It was one of those fancy ones, with a fully equipped kitchen, breakfast nook, shower, and plenty of sleeping room for all of us. This traveling luxury made road trips way more fun than my mom's station wagon. We could sit at the table, play cards, or lounge on her parents' bed in the back to watch a movie or two to make the time pass by. Towering above the other cars, I felt like queen of the highway.

Megan's older brother, Michael, also got to bring a friend along. I remember sitting at the table on our way home, and we were all growing a bit bored from the long road trip, so her brother and his friend came up with an activity: they were going to test us to see who was smarter.

"Hey, we have a game we want to play with y'all," Michael said.

I like games, I'm in.

"You both have to read passages that we select out of this book, and then we will quiz you on them to see how many questions you get right. The person who answers the most correctly wins."

I was thinking more like Uno.

Now, Megan was super smart. She never made under 100 on all her tests and quizzes without having to study—she was the perfect student. I wasn't far behind, but I had to work at every A I received.

Her brother, also a genius, who I'm pretty sure skipped at least one grade, was three years older than us, and it was his books we were being tested on. He made her read first, then took her to the back of the motorhome to quiz her. When it was my turn, all three of them sat and watched me read while one of them timed me. Why do smart people like doing school on the weekends? I was petrified. I was so concentrated on them focusing on me that I kept missing words and losing my place; I just wanted to hurry up and get it over with, so I skimmed the last bit and said, "Done!" *Hopefully, they think I'm smart because I read fast.*

They went back to grade my comprehension, and I could hear laughing in the background, which made me want to run and hide, but I was in a motorhome where hiding places are limited. My stomach turned into knots when her brother walked toward me with my results. I didn't want to know how poorly I had done compared to my whiz friend sitting next to me. Thankfully, I never knew. Turns out they made a pact not to tell me what I scored because they knew it would make me feel bad.

Out of the millions of memories I have growing up, why this one? Out of all the terrible middle school drama-filled days, bad breakups, and even through my parents' divorce, this memory sticks out like it happened yesterday. After all my accomplishments in life, the reading activity on a Sunday after college football in third grade *still* plagues me.

But why? Based on my grades, I was smart. I was a straight-A student in elementary and middle school and graduated with a 4.5 GPA. I was accepted into the University of Florida, one of the toughest state schools to get into. But through all of that, I suffered from impostor syndrome. I never felt like I belonged, like everyone was smarter than me, and I had no idea how I got there, sitting in the same classes, listening to the same professors.

I remember looking around in my organic chemistry class at all the diverse students from different cultures and backgrounds, thinking how much smarter they were than I and how high they must have scored on their ACTs or SATs. I must have slipped through the cracks.

My first day as a pharmaceutical representative was one of the scariest days of my life. Despite all the testing and training I had gone through, the thought of having a clinical conversation with a physician terrified me. Why did I think this job was for me? Physicians are brilliant human beings who know way more than I do. What could they possibly glean from me?

I wore my brand-new black suit with my first pair of expensive black heels, carrying my briefcase—my power suit. I walked into the office, with patients scattered about, nurses scurrying around, and felt a wave of intimidation. I immediately wanted to walk right back out. I had no choice but to hand my business card to the receptionist, take a seat, and pray she didn't call my name. It was a busy office, so maybe I could just wait a few minutes and then leave. I'll give it one more minute and then…

"Courtney?"

Oh no, she didn't forget. Now what do I do? Can I hide? No, shoot, she's looking right at me.

"Yes?" I say it like, "I'm here but also don't have to be if you'd prefer it that way."

"Dr. Pate will see you now."

Here we go. First day and probably not far from being the last. I walk through the door to find Dr. Pate standing there, looking at me, wearing the intimidating white doctor's coat, holding patient files. Oh, no! I've forgotten everything I had planned to say to him. It was something about my blood pressure medicine having a low side effect profile and being easily tolerated amongst a certain demographic. Too late now. I have to say something.

"Sular is free for military patients," I said. *That's all I got? Terrible.*

He looked at me and said, "Thank you, I'll keep that in mind."

Wow, I'm going straight to the top with those selling skills. Why did I lock up? I had been practicing my message repeatedly and even prepared for any objections he could challenge me with. I was ready.

Despite my blockbuster first day, I would go on to have substantial success in pharmaceutical sales. I was always at the top of the sales rankings, consistently being recognized for sales performance within my district and region, and even winning an award trip to Germany for my success selling a heart medication. Because of my impressive resume, I landed my job selling heart monitors, which was considered a promotion within the medical sales field.

I remember my husband and I were on the award trip I had won to Nevis, when one of the VPs approached me about taking a leadership position within the company. He said he saw me as a leader in my region and thought I could contribute much, given my lucrative sales career. I immediately turned him down. I didn't possess any more knowledge than anyone else in the salesforce. What would I teach them that they didn't already know? He had the wrong girl. I wanted to say, "yes," so badly, but heard, "you can't," which was the louder voice of the two.

My limiting beliefs are very apparent, and even more glaringly obvious is how much restraint I've allowed them to cause throughout my life. Like a Crane Claw Machine in an arcade, I've been trapped inside a glass cage, watching the world from inside, feeling as though I should be free, but not knowing how to escape. I'd get close many times, when someone would put quarters in the game, the claw would choose me, raise me up to the top, but at the last minute, something prevented me from being fully released, and I'd be dropped back into the sea of neon-colored stuffed animals.

During this transitional phase I was going through, I wondered who was responsible for my negative self-belief. By age 7, our limiting beliefs are believed to settle into our little minds and begin shaping our thoughts, attitudes, and behaviors, which stay with us for the rest of our lives. What happened at a young age that made me feel like I wasn't smart enough? How did I go from that little girl sitting in a blue chair holding onto the belief that the world was filled with limitless opportunity for me to an adult who felt the restraints of a hypothetical glass box? Who was the culprit?

Because I had been learning about our primal brains then, I knew they were ultimately responsible for our internal fear and doubt. As stated before, biology is responsible (or to blame) for many of our thoughts, choices, behaviors, and midlife crises. Because our brains haven't evolved much more from what they were 200,000 years ago, we are stuck applying the same brain functions that were adapted as purely a means for survival to a world that is largely run by technology and a civilization obsessed with material gains and status, leading to an increasing rate of depression, anxiety and stress. We are evolutionarily predisposed to live amongst a small tribe of 30 in an environment surrounded by nature, not an industrialized city inhabited by 2 million people in skyscrapers.[5] It's no wonder the majority of us

---

5 B. Grinde, "Happiness in the Perspective of Evolutionary Psychology," Journal of Happiness Studies: An Interdisciplinary Forum on Subjective Well-Being 3, no. 4 (2002): 331–354, https://doi.org/10.1023/A:1021894227295.

are exhausted and mentally overstimulated regularly; we are in constant combat with our innate human instincts.

It makes sense that the self-help industry has boomed in the last decade, as we as a people are searching for something. We have strayed so far from where we came from, and because of that, we have created this internal battle from within, leaving us confused, depleted, and unhappy. We are totally out of sync.

I believe we as a civilization are on the brink of a major shift, a conscious awakening to the return of self and hopefully a bit of a societal rewind.

I knew the biology behind my own negative self-talk; I knew it was out of survival, the strongest driver in our brains to this day. So, why was I still allowing these primal thoughts to dictate my reality?

I began spending hours and days trying to uncover what exactly happened in my early childhood years that had such a profound impact later in life. Around this time, I met my friend Abby for coffee, and she mentioned that everyone has some degree of childhood trauma. When I think of the word 'trauma', I think of a dramatic life experience that changes you forever, which hadn't happened to me, or else I wouldn't be in this purgatory I was in. I would know what caused my self-deprecation.

"I don't have trauma, though," I responded.

"Trauma isn't always obvious to us; it could be something we have buried and put out of our conscious minds. It doesn't have to be some big event, like an accident or assault; trauma is any experience that negatively impacts us and changes how we perceive ourselves and the world. These events can be 'small' and are often dismissed because they are perceived to 'not be a big deal' to most people."

This brought on a whole new project for me. At the time of this coffee date, I was in search of my highest potential. I knew I had a unique gift to give to the world, but I also knew I still had a lot of work to do internally. I had held onto my limiting beliefs for so long that I allowed them to bury my strengths and greatness in a dormant grave. I slowly saw that these thoughts had impacted my life, circumstances, outcomes, and reality, and I wanted to stop them once and for all. I no longer wanted to be caged by them, and knew to break free, I had to resurrect their origin.

Abby recommended uncovering my inner child through guided meditations. Later that day, at home, I grabbed my phone, went into our dark upstairs office, shut the door, and sat down on the bed. I went to my app for meditation and selected one on seeking your inner child. I was warned that these could be emotional. This one absolutely followed suit.

If you've ever done a guided meditation, you know there is a lot of grounding and breath work at the beginning, and then it gets into the guts of the meditation. After the initial setup, I was told to put myself in a vast meadow, with a large tree off in the distance. Walking toward it, I saw a little girl standing under this grand tree with sprawling branches, creating a beautiful green canopy of shade. It was me, a younger version of myself, and I was told to choose my age. I saw myself at age 7.

This image of myself popped into my head, where I was in 1st grade. There stood a little girl who exuded magical energy for life, with a sparkle in her eyes, but as I got closer, I noticed a dimness in her spirit. I went up to her and just hugged her, held her for a long while, and whispered in her little ear, "I love you. You are such a special person, and you will go on to do amazing things. I will always be right here for you. Never forget that." It makes me cry while I remember how much that child needed to hear that. I had made her wait too long.

As I emerged from my meditation, I felt lighter. I had been carrying this heavy load of limits throughout life, and finally began to release them from myself. I felt like a brand-new person, one who wasn't being controlled by her thoughts. My inner child meditation showed me what I needed to address with myself, what I needed to hear from what could only come from me. No one else could give me what I needed to move forward, but me.

But what surprised me the most was that I had begun slowly pulling the curtains away to reveal that it was me the whole time. I was a pink-stuffed bear in the claw machine at the arcade, and my thoughts were the glass container. That's what they did all my life: *contained* me. They prevented me from truly experiencing the world as we all intend to, stunting my potential and confidence.

First, let's back up. I cannot place the entire blame on myself, nor the terrible, timed trial reading test in a motorhome on the interstate when I was 9. No, this was an accumulation of a series of events that led to my chronic limiting beliefs. Micro events, if you will—not big enough to anchor a solid memory, but heavy enough to add to my limit load, or my trauma. I believe this is how it happened for me, maybe for all of us. When we're little, we absorb everything like sponges—every emotion, every memory, every compliment, every insult we embed into our subconscious. Because the strongest driver in our primal brains is survival, we hold onto negative experiences way more than positive ones, a function that used to keep us alive, but now, it does the opposite: it keeps us from *living*.

Unknowingly, I had chosen to listen to these words over and over throughout my life. I didn't know at the time that they lived in my subconscious, born from our drive to survive, away from danger, and what's more, I didn't realize they weren't real. They weren't facts. As I researched more about these mental thieves, I saw just how much they played a part in my daily life.

I could have been a regional manager. The VP of sales was offering it to me on a silver platter. Instead, I chose to allow the belief that I wasn't smart enough to take control of my career mobility. I stayed in the same exact spot for 12 years at the same company because of a lie I told myself. Every thought, perception, and feeling is a choice. I had allowed limiting beliefs to hold me back from pursuing different dreams, and now, I sought revenge.

I vividly remember sitting down to create my first digital course, "The Winning Mindset of Sales." It's about how to have long-term success in sales by adopting certain mindsets and behaviors; it was born out of what I saw the industry needed when I was in sales. Each day, for several months, I'd sit down at my desk to add more content to the modules, and with every stroke of the keyboard, I'd hear, "Who do you think you are? You think you can actually sell a course? You don't have the credentials, so no one will buy this. You are wasting your time." Creating the material for this course wasn't hard because I found it all so interesting and knew it was something people, not only in sales but everywhere, needed to hear. I poured my heart into making it as engaging and interactive as possible, also not dull. The hardest part of the process was silencing that negative inner voice telling me I wasn't good enough. I was writing the course content portion on limiting beliefs, and at the same time, fighting my way past my own.

These limiting beliefs were different, though. As loud as they were and as frequent as I heard them, they didn't carry the same weight as they had my whole life. I had to intentionally acknowledge each one and then brush them aside, knowing they were there to pull me back into my comfort zone, the safe zone. I was doing something I'd never dreamed I'd be doing. The words still hurt, they were still mean, but I had pulled their masks off to reveal what they truly were: little impostors from the past under the guise of my reality. But they weren't real, and I didn't have to listen to them this time.

Six months later, I had a complete 5-module online course and a beautifully designed website. For the first time, I could sit in awe of what I had accomplished. I never would or could have imagined *I*, the same person who always believed that everyone in the room was smarter and would never want to hear what I had to say, created something I'd soon introduce to the world. My untapped potential was being brought to the surface, and I was there to grab it. I fell in love with the word 'create'. I created something.

I wanted to go back and tell my 2nd-grade self what we had achieved. I felt so connected to that innocent feeling of being whatever I wanted to be—only now, it was actually happening. I wanted to show the crushed 9-year-old in the motorhome how far we had come to wash away all the shame she carried for all those years after, to tell her she would have people everywhere reading her passages of hope...without a stopwatch.

These courses grew into in-person workshops, and I remember speaking in my second one, teaching a room full of execs how to incorporate visualization techniques to reach goals. I stood there for a moment watching the people in the room, engaged, consumed with the material I was presenting, never taking their eyes off me, and hanging onto every word like I was giving them the secrets to buried treasure. The excitement, passion, and love I felt as I presented were feelings I had felt before, but not on that level. I felt full of life and energy, like I could burst into beams of light at any minute. These are the exact feelings I wrote down early in my journey to purpose that I wanted to feel each day. I finally lived those words, to feel like I was beginning to live as my higher self and seek my highest potential.

The craziest part about all of this isn't that I accomplished something I never knew possible, but that it all stemmed from my *thoughts*. Because I became aware of each limiting belief that crept into my mind, I became more familiar with them. Then, they gradually lost credibility or value one by one, like inflation. As time went on, without even realizing it, I began stepping out of my comfort zone and taking risks, both of which were led by passion and purpose.

Don't Believe Everything You Think

When you start your visualization exercise, you will hear, "*that's impossible and unrealistic*," which is fear trying to sabotage your goals. To block these feelings, we first must make ourselves aware of them.

We all have fears and doubts. These are mainly based on previous experiences, priming us to avoid bad or harmful situations. A bad experience has twice the effect on the brain as a positive one, which explains why we take losses so hard and don't celebrate the "small" wins enough. It also explains perception, which can be a tricky little monster. A perception is a person's own unique view of the world based on past experiences. No one on this entire planet can go through life sharing another's exact perception, because no two people have had the exact same life experiences—this proves that perception is, in fact, not reality. However, how one perceives something significantly impacts one's reality, so it is essential to choose the right perception to have positive outcomes and life experiences. And you guessed it—this is yet another point where, if you allow them, fear and doubt can take the driver's seat.

One day, my daughter, who was ten at the time, came home from school and, like every day, unfolded all the events that had ensued. Recess had been tough lately. With a large group of girls, there were always feelings getting hurt, it seemed.

"My friends ignored me on the playground today," she said. "Or, maybe they just didn't hear me."

I loved this so much because it gave me the opportunity to explain what perceptions were.

"Those are two different perceptions," I said.

"What are perceptions?" she asked.

"Perceptions are an accumulation of past memories or experiences, and sometimes we allow them to dictate our present," I said.

"Well, which one is the right one?" she asked.

"Which one makes you feel better?"

"That they just didn't hear me," she answered.

"Then that's the right one," I said.

If my daughter had perceived this situation as her friends ignoring her, her day would have been ruined. Instead, she chose to see it as an innocent mistake. As a result, she was able to move past it.

You always have the opportunity to choose a perspective that aligns with your goals and aspirations. By thinking in terms of the worst-case scenario, we are strengthening those negative neural pathways. So, the next time you feel yourself perceiving a situation negatively, stop and try viewing it from a more positive, empowering angle. Don't let negative past experiences dictate your present or future; you are the creator of your life, and you have infinite power to live to your fullest potential. With that comes being more deliberate in your thoughts and actions.

Our brains are risk-averse to keep us out of harm's way, but they can also keep us stagnant. If we become aware of this, we can work on managing these limiting thoughts and moving closer to our goals.

Fear and doubt also reveal themselves in unfamiliar situations. Unfamiliarity triggers fear in our brains, which flips on our survival mode. When this happens, we retreat, not seizing opportunities or stepping outside our comfort zones. We're stagnant.

One way to prevent this is through visualization. If you can successfully visualize yourself sitting in the chair facing your interviewer—or the vast crowd while you take the stage to deliver a speech—right down to the clothes you're wearing and what you see and hear in that moment, you are familiarizing your brain with this new territory, taking it out of the limiting, survival mode and into "I can" mode. Remember, your brain can't decipher between a powerful visualization and reality, so if you practice this repeatedly, it will perceive it as "familiar," and override the doubt phase altogether, leaving you with the confidence to seize any high-stakes opportunity.

Let's look at how the subconscious and conscious minds work. Your subconscious mind is comprised of memories and experiences, and it feeds this information to your conscious mind, which influences your interactions, perceptions, behavior, and ultimately your reality. It has a lot of influence: 95 percent of our thoughts are subconscious, leaving only five percent of our cognitive activity stemming from our conscious minds. That's pretty unbelievable. Your subconscious is like the puppet master to your conscious puppet, and if fear and doubt are the lead characters, then you're allowing them to run the show, *your* show.

This proves the notion that your thoughts affect your reality. To reach any goal or have a desired outcome, you must influence your subconscious mind first.

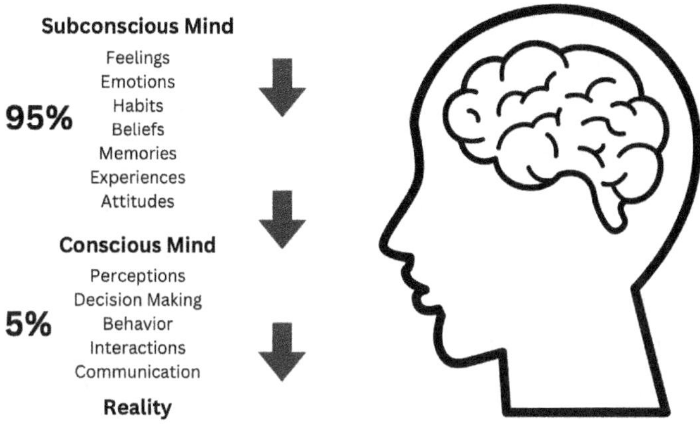

How many times have you set a hefty goal, but something held you back? You heard, "*You're not smart enough,*" or "*that's unrealistic.*" That was fear and doubt. Let's take the famous New Year's Resolution of getting in shape. You buy new clothes, a gym membership, and maybe even a treadmill to facilitate the new you. In the first few weeks, you're prioritizing exercise and eating healthy, determined to hit your fitness goals. But then, after about a month or two…your motivation and sense of excitement dwindle, and you find yourself working out twice a week, then once, and then soon not at all. You've lost all stamina. This is because you skipped a step: you never influenced your subconscious, and your primal brain took over.

When we set a goal, we task our brains with changing behavior, which they dislike. When we try to change our behavior to reach a goal, we ask our brains to do something out of the ordinary, out of our comfort zones, signaling to our brains, "danger."

So, when we do the unexpected, our brains trigger the fight or flight response and negative self-talk to keep us safe. This is where most people stop in their goal-setting process, because they aren't aware of these limiting beliefs and are falsely led back to the life to which they're accustomed. These emotions are the antithesis of growth, the potholes or roadblocks that aim to end your journey.

My friend Megan is incredibly successful in sales. She's been in the medical sales industry for 13+ years and has grown her business year after year, which only a few of the top reps in any company can do. Now, anyone who understands sales knows this is super challenging because sales goals increase with each year of success. To have continued success, you have to find new customers and grow enormously every year without fail. It's one of the main reasons for burnout in the industry, because you really can't enjoy your accomplishments if you know you will face a higher goal for the following year.

Megan, however, is able not only to hit the goal each year but exceed it, seemingly with ease. When I asked her how she does it, knowing she faces the same challenges we all faced at the time, she said, "I win because nothing is telling me I can't." She told me she's no different from anyone else and has the same struggles, but she chooses not to fail.

"It's literally a choice," she said. "I choose not to feel sorry for myself. I choose the people I surround myself with, and I choose to turn the voices telling me I can't do something off."

The difference between successful reps like Megan and the rest of the sales organization is their inner communication: They choose which thoughts to listen to and watch what they say to themselves. It's not that these reps are more talented or have better selling skills than anyone else—it's that they choose to always have a winning mindset, no matter the circumstance.

Choose Your Thoughts

Discovering and disposing of your limiting beliefs can profoundly transform your life. You gain clarity about the false narratives that hold you back by identifying them. Letting go of these beliefs frees you to adopt a more empowering mindset, fostering personal growth, confidence, and resilience. This shift enables you to pursue opportunities with an open mind, embrace challenges, and achieve goals that once seemed unattainable.

You can't reach your destination until you acknowledge and dispose of these limiting beliefs. Awareness is the first step of transformation—to block fear and doubt, we must become aware of them.

Let's Journal

Limiting beliefs don't have to be roadblocks. Once we identify and challenge these beliefs, we can rewrite narratives that no longer serve us. This journaling exercise will help you uncover the limiting beliefs shaping your decisions and replace them with empowering truths. Through reflection and intentional writing, you'll gain clarity, shift your mindset, and take a step closer to the limitless possibilities.

Write down a goal and then write down all the limiting beliefs that are preventing you from obtaining it. Ask yourself, "What's holding me back? What's stopping me?" Seeing this on paper will help you be fully aware of these thoughts, so the next time you hear them, you know exactly what they sound like, and eventually, you can control them and put them away.

For example, when I was in sales, my goal would look like this:

Goal: Reach $100K in sales by the end of the year

Limiting beliefs:

The amount is too high to obtain.

I don't have the skills necessary to reach that goal.

I don't have enough customers.

I don't have enough time to grow my customer base.

I'm scared that I won't make any commission if I don't reach that goal.

Write down everything that is holding you back and then take a minute to reflect. These subconscious limiting beliefs keep you from living the life you want. Now is the time to take control of these thoughts and set them free, so that you can live in your power instead.

I highly recommend doing this because it allows you to visibly see the thoughts on paper and bring them into reality. You see them, acknowledge them, and then let them go, resulting in a power shift. When you do this exercise, you're taking power away from your fear and doubt and disseminating it to your inner confidence.

I made it my mission to commit to the daily practice of realizing when I had a limiting belief and then disposing of it. You must be so incredibly aware of fear and doubt that you view them as almost tangible things you can feel and see, so you can remove them as easily as they come to you.

Once we recognize self-limiting beliefs, we can replace them with inspiring ones. Have you ever heard the phrase, "We pick our thoughts like we pick out our shoes in the morning"? It's true; we can combat each negative subconscious thought with a positive, more empowering one, and by doing so, we are reprogramming our brains to want the same things we do.

Our subconscious is what we create, so how we talk to ourselves is extremely important. Remember my successful colleague, Megan? She *chooses* to listen to the thoughts that support her goals and ignore the ones that try to block them. Let's copy Megan. Implement the following brain exercise whenever you feel fear and doubt creeping in. Each time you hear yourself about to say something negative, replace that thought with an empowering one. Write them down so you can practice repeating them regularly.

Instead of **"I can't do that,"** change it to
"I can do anything I put my mind to."

Instead of **"I'm not good enough,"** change it to
"I am capable of anything."

Instead of **"I wish I could get that job,"** change it to
"I look forward to the day I will enjoy my job."

Instead of **"I don't deserve this,"** change it to
"I am worthy of great things."

Instead of **"This won't work out,"** change it to
"But what if it does?"

When you're going through this, try not to use the word *want* because it carries the connotation that it's something you don't have. This is part of a scarcity mindset, discussed in the next chapter, and comes from a place of lack. If our subconscious is dictating our conscious thoughts, then we must trick our subconscious into thinking with an abundance mindset. You want to use phrases like "I look forward to…" because you must feel as though you already have it.

We now understand the importance of positive self-talk and how influential our subconscious thoughts are to our conscious awareness, but to put this into practice, repetition is required. The more our subconscious hears empowering thoughts, the more we increase our self-worth, driving us closer to our ultimate goal.

We can cultivate positive self-talk and incorporate it into our daily lives through mantras. This is something that I admit may be uncomfortable at first, but like anything else, with consistency, it becomes second nature. Write your mantras down and then say them out loud, whichever works for you. Here are some of my favorite mantras:

I am capable of great things.

I am smart enough.

I am inspiring.

I am prosperous.

I am constantly attracting abundance into my life.

I am grateful.

I am worthy of acquiring all that I ask for.

This process allows you and your brain to get on the same page and become more aligned, so both of you work towards the same goal. If you don't influence your subconscious when it comes to goal setting, you're working against 95% of your brain… and your primal brain, resulting in odds not being in your favor.

Let's Meditate

As my dear friend Abby said, "We all have trauma." What she means is we all have generational trauma. Generational trauma is the inherited energetic imprint of unresolved pain, fear, and emotional wounds passed down through family lines. It is believed that trauma experienced by ancestors leaves an energetic residue within the collective soul of a family, shaping patterns, behaviors, and emotional responses in descendants. This inheritance isn't just genetic or psychological—it's also spiritual, manifesting as karmic cycles or ancestral burdens that repeat until acknowledged and healed. Meditation lets us break these cycles for ourselves and our entire lineage, past and future.

This is my favorite meditation to start the healing process: Close your eyes and take a deep breath in, feeling the air fill your lungs, and exhale slowly, letting go of any tension in your body. Picture yourself standing on a serene beach at sunrise, the soft golden light of the sun casting a warm glow over the sand. The sound of gentle waves lapping at the shore soothes your mind, and a light breeze carries the scent of the sea. As you walk along the shore, you notice a radiant figure ahead, emanating warm and loving energy. This is your Higher Self—the wisest, most empowered version of you. As you approach, they greet you with a compassionate smile and say, "You are ready to heal, to release the burdens you have carried for so long."

Your Higher Self guides you to a quiet spot near the water, holding a glowing bowl of light. Inside, you see shadowy orbs, each one representing a limiting belief passed down through your lineage. Your Higher Self hands you the first orb, and as you hold it, you intuitively recognize its weight—a fear of scarcity, of never being enough. You walk to the water's edge and gently place the orb into the waves, watching as it dissolves into pure light, carried away by the ocean. With each release, you feel lighter. One by one, you acknowledge each orb, recognizing unworthiness, guilt, or shame patterns that no longer serve you. Each belief is met with love and compassion, and as you let them go, your Higher Self whispers affirmation: "You are abundant. You are worthy. You are free."

The water becomes clearer and brighter as the final orb dissolves, reflecting the light within you. You feel a profound sense of relief and liberation. Your Higher Self places their hands over your heart, infusing you with healing energy and reminding you that you are not alone in this journey. In that moment, you sense the presence of your ancestors—not as carriers of trauma, but as sources of strength, wisdom, and love. They offer you blessings: resilience, courage, creativity, and the freedom to live fully. You accept these gifts with gratitude, feeling them fill every corner of your being.

As you turn to walk back along the beach, you feel lighter, freer, and more aligned with your true self. The sun's warmth touches your skin, a reminder of the light you now carry within. When you are ready, take a deep breath, bring your awareness back to the present moment, and open your eyes, knowing you have begun a powerful journey of healing, not just for yourself, but for those who came before you and those who will follow.

As we heal the wounds of the generations before us, we must also turn inward to the part of ourselves that first learned these patterns—our inner child. Healing this part of ourselves ensures that we do not continue carrying these wounds forward. With that in mind, let's explore our next meditation: Inner Child Healing.

Healing your inner child allows you to address unresolved emotions, unmet needs, and painful experiences from your past that influence your behaviors, relationships, and self-perception. The inner child represents the part of you that carries the memories, emotions, and beliefs formed during childhood, including both joyful and traumatic experiences. When this part of you remains wounded or neglected, it can manifest as self-doubt, fear, or destructive patterns in adulthood. You create space for self-compassion, emotional release, and personal growth by nurturing and reconnecting with your inner child. This process helps you break free from limiting beliefs and develop healthier ways to relate to yourself and others, ultimately fostering a sense of wholeness and inner peace.

For this, sit or lie down comfortably, close your eyes, and take three deep breaths. Inhale deeply through your nose, hold for a moment, and exhale slowly through your mouth. With each breath, let go of any tension or stress and imagine yourself sinking deeper into relaxation. Visualize roots extending from your body into the ground below, anchoring you to the earth. Feel the stability and support of the earth beneath you, allowing it to ground and protect you during this journey. Imagine yourself walking down a peaceful path in nature. It could be a forest, a beach, or a meadow—wherever you feel safe and at ease. At the end of the path, you see a small, inviting door or gate. This is the entrance to your inner world. When you're ready, step through the door. Inside, you find yourself in a beautiful, safe space—a warm, comforting environment where your inner child feels completely secure. As you look around, you notice your younger self approaching you. This might be you at any age—whatever image feels most natural, or whichever age first comes to your mind. Observe your inner child's expression and energy. Notice how they feel and what they might need. Gently say, "Hello, I'm here to listen to you and support you. You are safe with me."

Sit with your inner child, allowing them to share anything they feel—words, emotions, or even silence.

If your inner child seems hurt or sad, imagine wrapping them in a warm, glowing light of love. Let this light flow from your heart to theirs. Say kind, reassuring words such as:

"I love you."

"You are enough just as you are."

"I am here to protect you."

Let your inner child know they are always with you, and you will continue to care for them. Imagine your inner child merging gently into your heart, where they will always be loved and protected. Slowly bring your awareness back to the door and step through, returning to the path. Walk back to the present moment, feeling grounded and whole. Take a deep breath and slowly open your eyes. Wiggle your fingers and toes to reconnect with your physical body. Spend a moment reflecting on the experience. You may choose to write down any insights or emotions in a journal.

Final Thoughts

Moving forward, I want you to be aware of negative self-talk and limiting beliefs. When you partake in a visualization exercise or think about your life goals, you will notice that fear and doubt will creep in. Each time you feel constrained when it comes to your vision, know it's those limiting beliefs trying to talk you out of it. If you know these impostors, you can silence them with empowering thoughts. The more you do this practice, the closer you will be to accomplishing your goals.

Remember this: even if you don't fully believe what you're telling yourself, you will gradually turn your mantras into beliefs, influencing your subconscious and shaping your reality. The most successful people I know have mastered their thoughts. It's important to understand that this skill is available to anyone who practices it. Remember: if you're not controlling your subconscious, then your subconscious controls you.

By utilizing these practices daily, you will be armed with the tools to overcome your detours and potholes to continue your journey to greatness. It's important to realize that, with each step towards your goal, you must anticipate discomfort and negative self-talk. This is normal and crucial for personal expansion and growth, a stepping into the discomfort of the unknown. When you feel this, keep going (maybe even thank fear and doubt for showing up), because what's on the other side is the life you've always been searching for.

CHAPTER 4

Abundance

When you are grateful, fear disappears, and abundance appears. –Tony Robbins

"Abundance" is a funny word. I admit it took me a while to understand it completely. We usually use this term when it comes to money, wealth, and prosperity—things vastly sought after, and that's the ironic part because "abundance" is none of those things.

Some naturally think abundantly. Some people are just born happy, no matter their circumstances. Do you know these people? They may have a lot or a little. It doesn't matter; they're just always happy. I've watched this small segment of our population throughout my life, and I've concluded that their happiness is independent of how much money they make or what kind of house they live in. They are happy, rich or poor, in challenging or easy times. Their constant state of mind is contentment.

I was not one of the lucky ones who were born this way. I'm not one of these people.

Let's go back for a minute. I grew up in a middle-class family, my dad worked for the family business, and my mom stayed home. We had everything we needed, but not a whole lot extra. We weren't the family taking ski trips each winter or going on cruises during the summer. We didn't ride in airplanes or own passports; we didn't even know people left the country. But my brother and I didn't know anything different. How I wish I could go back to not knowing.

We spent our summer days on Pensacola Beach at my grandparents' beach house, where the whole family would meet for a full day of grilling, inner tubing, and water skiing. My cousins and I would swim for hours in the Santa Rosa Sound, splashing, racing each other, and sometimes just floating lazily, gazing up at the sky. The Sound's sandy bottom was visible through the crystal-clear water, providing the perfect backdrop for our underwater adventures. Those moments, surrounded by family and nature's beauty, remain my fondest memories, capturing the essence of carefree, sun-soaked summer days. I never wanted those days to end and always wished the sun could stay up for a few more minutes, to get one more giggle-filled inner tube ride in before dark. I remember thinking how lucky I was to get to do those things, being so grateful for my life and the people in it.

We gathered at my grandparents' house for Sunday dinners with the family. Their home was a sanctuary of love, laughter, and the aroma of roast beef in the crock pot. The dining table, covered with a familiar seasonal tablecloth, was always set hours before we arrived, just awaiting the playful banter and entertaining stories that would soon surround it. The dining room served as a harbor of comical conversations as we all squeezed around the table, sharing the week's happenings and enjoying each other's company. To this day, the most I've ever laughed was around that table, the deep, belly laugh that resulted in tears and lack of oxygen. I loved starting the week with those dinners, with a sense of fullness and serenity. Even as young as 8, I knew these Sunday evenings served a far greater purpose than sharing a meal with loved ones.

There is something within these memories that I have held to a higher regard well into middle age, not even meaning to. The ones I've clung to aren't shiny and glamorous; they certainly don't seem unusual for any family to experience. I can't remember what Santa brought me when I was ten or what birthday presents I got at my first slumber party. Isn't it funny how we didn't recognize the material things back then? We didn't care about where our friends lived or who had what. As children, we weren't yet tainted by societal measures; our primary focus was having fun, and we chose our friends based on who could deliver it. It's almost like God gifts us with blinders when we're young, providing us a good decade of blissful ignorance and blithe wonderment before exposing us to the world of material girls.

As I got older, I recognized the differences between myself and others. Some of my friends had two-story houses, which I had always wanted (I called them "upstairs-downstairs homes"), swimming pools, and their parents drove newer cars. Little by little, I started to compare myself, my clothes, my shoes, and my looks to others. Why did Jenny have long, thick, beautiful hair, when I had short, thin, and limp hair? Why did Katie always have new shoes while I wore the same white Keds every day? And why can't we have a minivan?

As we age, we start comparing ourselves to others, often measuring our successes and failures against the benchmarks set by those around us. We are more aware of the world than when we were young. From that carefree time, we slowly inherit society's dictations of happiness, which contradict those we experience in our youth, the genuine abundance that doesn't come with price tags. As time passes, we become more susceptible to feelings of inadequacy and jealousy as we perceive others as more accomplished, happier, or fulfilled. These comparisons can overshadow our achievements and erode our self-esteem, fostering a sense of rivalry or resentment.

I, although not proud of it, have the perfect example of this. It was a hot July Saturday, and my husband, children, and I were having a lazy start to the day. As we were tossing out ideas of what we wanted to do, it became glaringly obvious that none of us could agree. My husband wanted to go to a pool, but the kids and I thought that sounded boring. My son and I wanted to go to the beach, but my daughter argued it was too hot.

Then, I said, "I wish we had a boat. That would solve all our problems."

This encouraged my daughter to respond, "Yeah, everyone else we know has one, why don't we?"

Annoyed that we didn't have one, I threw an internal tantrum. I pictured everyone out on their boats, bobbing through the emerald waters, seeing dolphins jump and sting rays glide while we stared at our four walls. Why did I quit my job? If I hadn't, we surely would have a boat by now. But I wanted to serve a higher purpose—that used to sound so good, but now it was tasting a bit stale.

I had no recent business opportunities, and none were on the horizon. I heard a lot of "Yeah, that sounds great, I'll get back to you," which led to many dead ends. I wondered if I should start applying for jobs. My future, our future, was hanging in limbo because I didn't know when or if I would make progress with my coaching program. In that moment, I craved the old job that brought me financial peace. The fact was, I wasn't sleeping, was always anxious, and grew depressed over my decision to walk away from a six-figure salary.

I felt sorry for myself and my family, and angry. We should have a boat; we live on the Gulf Coast, where there's not much to do during summer except be on the water.

At the same time, I looked out of my kitchen window to see my neighbor's brand-new, 23-foot, sparkling, white, center console boat being delivered right in front of our house.

My husband laughed, "Oh, great timing."

As I peered out of the window, I saw a big truck backing in the new boat, the new owners excitedly waving him in the driveway. The family rushed out to look at it. The little children climbed on board, bouncing with anticipation to take it on the maiden voyage. They all looked…very…happy.

I couldn't help but laugh too, but at myself. I knew it was the Universe's way of checking me, sending me a sign that I was out of line, reminding me that I had all that I needed. I stopped in my tracks and decided to think of everything I had in front of me: my husband, two children, our health, and our "upstairs-downstairs" home. Many people would love to have all those things, and I needed to better focus on what I had instead of the lack thereof.

It's difficult for most people to think in abundance, unless you're one of those few born with the abundance gene I mentioned at the beginning of the chapter. The abundance principle is the idea that there are enough resources for everyone, and that someone else's success does not take away from your own. When we go through life using an abundance mindset, we concentrate on what we *do* have, not what we don't, and look at others with more as inspiration, not something to envy. When we utilize the abundant mindset, we attract more abundance into our lives. Sounds so easy...

Children are great at this, but adults? Not so much. Especially today, with the infinite access to social media, the constant exposure to curated glimpses of others' lives, which look newer, shinier, and prettier than your own, makes it challenging to appreciate our unique journeys and progress.

You could have the day of your dreams, only for social media to completely end it all in seconds. You could think you're killing it in the motherhood department, waking up early to make lunches so everyone gets to school on time, just to see another mom's post on her homemade lunches that include fresh, colorful organic fruits and veggies, and sandwiches cut into shapes served in plastic-free containers. Processed foods nowhere to be seen. Have you ever noticed how many vacations are documented? You're so blinded by the white, sandy beaches, palm trees, and relaxed smiles that you can't see the fights, stress, and lack of sleep that led up to that picture. Social media is a breeding ground for feelings of insufficiency, highlighting the lack mindset we all operate under. Most people are unfortunately accustomed to grading themselves based on what they have compared to others, fostering a sense of competition for nicer houses, shinier cars, and impressive vacations, all of which are a false sense of abundance. When we place weight on outward things such as material items, we immediately put ourselves into the lack mindset of wanting more instead of focusing on what we have in the present.

I teach the importance of the abundance mindset, but I wasn't practicing it. I knew that to make strides professionally, I had to think about how far I've come, what I've accomplished, and what

I've created. Yes, it was progressing slower than I wanted it to, but still progressing, and that's what I had to keep telling myself. Most entrepreneurs fail because of the unknown—it's scary, terrifying, and comes without a timeline. Many of us could tolerate the 'unknown' if we knew the duration, but most of us can't live in this state without a clear path ahead.

It's very easy to think abundantly when life is easy, you see the fruits of your labor, and the things you so desperately want aren't out of reach. Do you know what's hard, like, really hard? Thinking in abundance when you don't have any of that. When life isn't easy, you face challenges, and dream of a day when life gets fun again. But perhaps that's the most crucial time to practice it. Like the blatant boat sign, thinking in terms of abundance places us back to when those things didn't matter—when we wore blinders.

As human adults, we nail the scarcity mindset, and I will blame it on our ancestors. We operate under this mindset out of survival, as it's our primal brain's effort to prevent us from harm. Its main objective is risk avoidance. Our ancestors were hunters, gatherers, and survivalists; for example, they were scared if they didn't have enough food. They lived in fear of starvation. Their primal brains told them to hoard what they had, to keep it safe from others who may be seeking food too, creating a climate of envy and isolation. Now, because our survival instincts are so strong, lack of food is our focus, our main thought: not having enough, what we lack. We were quite literally living in a world of scarcity. So, to stay alive, we had to act accordingly—fearing what we lacked helped keep us alive. By design, when we navigate under this lack mindset, it's impossible for us to think of anything other than what we don't have, preventing us from seeing opportunities right in front of us. Because we're in this limited mindset, we get stuck.

When I started my coaching business, I hadn't received a paycheck for two years since quitting my sales job. To say I was feeling very anxious (desperate) for a paid gig is an understatement. I learned not to fall too hard for the empty promises, like when your high school crush would flirt just enough to get your hopes up, right before forgetting your name. I had about 45 of those in the first three months I launched my course. I would get so close, then communication would fall off a cliff.

What was I doing wrong? Every morning, the first thing I would do is look at my email inbox number. You know how it shows on the outside of the icon? 11. That number remained for months, with the only time it reached 12 being when I received an automated email. I was obviously doing something wrong, so I decided to change my strategy and work on myself.

I was very much experiencing the effects of the Law of Attraction, which incorporates the Quantum physics theory that like attracts like.

Everything in the Universe is made up of energy: the clothes you're wearing, the clouds above, even our feelings and emotions have energy. And everything that is comprised of matter or energy has different vibrational frequencies, ranging from high to low. Because like attracts like, high-vibrational frequencies attract other high-vibrational frequencies, and the same for low-vibrational frequencies. When it comes to our thoughts, feelings, and emotions, we get back what we put out into the world. So, just by changing our thoughts, we can change how we feel, the energetic field around us, and most importantly, our vibrational frequencies that ultimately change our realities.

This opened my eyes to the mistakes that led to me losing that big hospital account: I was living, working, eating, sleeping, and breathing the scarcity mindset. Every conversation and interaction I had with customers echoed my fear of losing business. I concentrated so heavily on what would happen if I lost the account, my bonuses, and sales ranking that I lost sight of my sole reason for my employment: to help people. I wasn't there just to help extend the lives of heart patients. I was there to help physicians formulate diagnoses, treatment plans, and surgeries. I was there to educate nurses and staff to prepare patients for their next steps. I had built a community within that hospital for years.

Had I stopped to see how much value I had delivered to my customers, how much business I had grown, and how many people I had already helped, I believe I would have come from a place of confidence, security, and collaboration. I would have positioned myself as a resource to my offices, not someone popping in to check if they were giving my business to the competition. The fact was, I was scared of my competitor, and I allowed that to override my strengths and accomplishments, inevitably sabotaging my career.

And I found myself in a familiar spot: fear. By thinking about the business I didn't have, I was thinking about lack, which was causing me to attract just that: lack of business (along with lack of sleep, peace, and sanity). That day, I decided to get back to my morning ritual, a combination of prayer, meditation, and writing in my gratitude journal. But this time, I wasn't asking for abundance; I asked for the opportunity to *see* my abundance. To attract more, I had to hold gratitude for all the goodness that I had in my life in that very moment, focus on how I wanted to feel each day, and have faith that everything was going to work out. It brought me a sense of peace and confidence.

I finally understood—you can't receive *abundance* until you feel *abundant*. It's a feeling, not something you hold in your hand. If like attracts like, then I had been very unattractive to abundance. I needed to replicate feelings of immense gratitude I'd experienced in the past, preferably when I was a child, back when I was fully submersed in the present and didn't want for anything, back to the days of Sunday suppers and saltwater swims.

Gratitude! Why didn't that occur to me before? Holding gratitude, even when things aren't perfect, raises your vibration immediately. That's what the Universe responds to: your vibrational energy.

From then on, I began my prayers by thanking my team for all the guidance they had given me thus far in my journey, all the support and signs, my God-given stubbornness, and my husband's deep-rooted belief in me. With a grateful heart, I'd thank God for the obstacles he placed in my way, which allowed me to build the knowledge, resiliency, and grit necessary for accomplishing my goals. I thanked Him for instilling in me this purpose to serve and the ability to carry that duty out into the world, which allowed me to see the world as abundant despite my setbacks. I shifted my mindset from fearful to fearless, had a boost in my confidence, and began to look at my future, although uncertain, with optimism. The more I turned my thoughts from worry to gratitude, the more my self-confidence strengthened, my self-worth skyrocketed, and I began to realize the life of my dreams. A sense of calming determination washed over me. I could sleep again.

That next day, I woke up to the number 13 in my inbox. I had received two emails from substantial companies asking me to hold a workshop for their employees. I looked up, said a silent, "Thank you," and wrote in my gratitude journal.

Embrace Gratitude to Attract Abundance

Thinking in terms of abundance is perhaps the exact opposite of what we're taught in the Corporate America sales industry. We are conditioned to seek out new customers and opportunities and to take them from competitors because this is the definition of a "win." We are trained not to like the competition because we want what they have, and each success they experience takes away from our own.

The problem is that we think in limiting terms. When we do this, we've closed ourselves off to seeking new opportunities and taking risks—basically, we're telling our subconscious to flip on survival mode. When we're in this, we're not looking for forward momentum to drive our potential; we're staying still. We're letting fear take the wheel, and by doing so, we're strengthening those negative neural pathways, making us resistant to change and growth.

You can shift from a scarcity mindset to an abundance mindset through the act of giving. Abundant thinkers generously give their time, resources, and money to others without expecting reciprocity or anything in return. They believe that because the world has endless possibilities, they will reach their goals through helping others.

Researchers Bob Cross and Karen Dillon conducted a study on high performers, a project initially intended to better understand how certain people were able to be more effective at work, for a sustained period. They interviewed 300 people designated as high performers by their organizations, but learned that most of these high performers were highly stressed out and overwhelmed. They also found that about 10% of this group were not only able to be high achievers but also rise above the stress and handle the same stress better than most of their colleagues. They were called the "Ten Percenters."

What was remarkable was that though the "Ten Percenters" made good money, had nice things, took nice vacations, it wasn't the focus of their identity. Instead, they had a sense of purpose in their lives separate from money or things. When asked what some of their sources of purpose were, they often had to do with helping others in the form of giving. The study showed that giving to others, even in small ways, can generate a palpable sense of purpose, and that activities that transcend self-fulfillment via material gains lead to greater well-being over time.

Try to apply this to your everyday life. In the workplace, for example, try not to always go into a situation with the objective of getting something out of it. Whether it's a customer or colleague, ask yourself, *"What can I give to this person/office that would help make their lives easier? How can I help them today?"* At home, try to carve out some time for a loved one, help a neighbor who lives alone, or donate to a deserving charity. These seemingly small things will mean a whole lot more to others, and in turn, you will be shown abundance.

When you're in the abundance mindset, your creative genius flows, fueling your self-esteem and confidence; by doing so, others are drawn to you. People want to help, work, and collaborate with you because your energy is infectious. You're resilient, and you can persevere through the hard times because change is not something you fear—rather, you embrace it, because with change comes progress and transformation.

By focusing on what you have versus what you lack, you're creating a more attractive "you". For example, if you're wanting to go after a promotion, you may have thoughts like, *"Why would they choose me over someone with more tenure?"* or *"I don't have enough accolades on my resume to compete with other more accomplished colleagues."*

This is the lack mindset, which places you back into that limited belief system. Instead of concentrating on what you don't have, think about the qualities you possess that make you a desirable candidate for any job promotion. Try, *"My years of experience make me an asset to this position."* You want to change those limiting beliefs into opportunities.

The sales industry is notorious for breeding a scarcity mindset because many salespeople are competitive. Many even have sports backgrounds that help cultivate their competitive nature. That's the reason many are hired for sales positions—because sales, like sports, is competitive. We get ourselves into trouble by channeling our competitiveness through fear and jealousy—as we've already said, these limiting beliefs amplify the "I can't" voice.

I know it's hard to be happy for a competitor when they experience success—believe me, I was never good at it—but we need to change that narrative and instead tell ourselves, *"I'm happy for their success, but I know there's enough to go around, and I'm excited to experience my next big win."* Instead of letting your competitor's news ruin your day, look at it from a positive or inspiring perspective. Ask yourself: *"How did they do it? How can I learn from them? How can I apply this to my daily work?"* When we do this, we are moving past the limiting beliefs of doubt and closer to what we want to manifest.

Carrying gratitude throughout the day is challenging because no day is perfect, and at some point, there will be an obstacle to overcome. However, despite these circumstances, remaining in a state of gratitude opens you up to an abundant mindset and sets you up for successful goal attainment.

Embracing gratitude leads to less stress and a greater sense of self by forcing you to remain present. No matter your situation, you can always find a reason to practice gratitude. Look at your life: if you're able to sit down, read this book, and work on yourself, you're already far better off than most of the world. Think about your goals, accomplishments, and the life you've built—by doing this, you automatically start blocking out fear and doubt, because you can't have two thoughts at once. You can't be in a complete state of gratitude while being sad or mad, which is why gratitude improves your overall wellness.

Your situation may not be preferable, or a part of your plan, but you're right where you need to be. If not for life's challenges, you wouldn't have been led to this moment, so reflect on that, and then seek gratitude for that inner voice of inspiration telling you to go for your dreams. You must honor where you are and where you are going to manifest any goal. This is where the magic happens: when you are seeking something more, while being completely grateful for where you are now.

At the age of 39, I'm just now understanding this concept. I've always compared myself to others: what trips they were going on, what house they lived in, what cars they could afford. If I could manage to do the same things or possess comparable luxury items, I would be "happy." I have since realized this "happiness" that I achieved was temporary, attaching my self-worth to external things alone. Houses become outdated, cars turn into older models—it's just a matter of time before you're back in the same scenario of wishing for more. You will never find true gratitude or happiness through material things.

Please note that there is nothing wrong with setting a goal for a tangible object, such as a house or car. Just know that acquiring this item is not fulfillment. Fulfillment is internal and long-lasting, while the excitement of material items is external and ephemeral. As we went over in Chapter 1, to create a long-lasting connection with your material goals, be sure to know your "why."

Remember in the last chapter when I said negative experiences are twice as powerful on the brain as positive ones? Well, practicing gratitude can reverse that by putting greater significance on happier moments instead of unsatisfactory ones.

When I started learning about true gratitude, I began each day by saying at least three things I felt gratitude for. This is not always easy, especially on the hard days when nothing seems to go your way, but I promise it's effective. After running through my list each day, I felt a shift in my mood—doing this exercise showed me how much I truly had. It transformed me into someone with an abundance mindset, even if I wasn't feeling particularly abundant that day. It brought me peace and calm, and afterwards, I was much more focused and motivated.

You can practice embracing gratitude in every aspect of your life, especially the ones that aren't your favorite. While working in my corporate career, I hated quarterly sales reports because they ate into the time I could spend calling on customers and growing my business. Still, I was home for hours working in front of my computer. I should have changed my perspective. I should have thought about the dedicated time I got to dive into my territory, performance, and trends. Each time I began my reports, I would start annoyed, but by the end, I felt accomplished as I gained tremendous insight. It allowed me to move forward with an action plan for potential customers and made my life easier.

When we first got our dog, I quickly realized the empty promises of responsibility my children had made when they begged for a dog, and that I would be the one to take him on his daily walks, amongst every other component of keeping a pet alive. But I grew tired of having this task hang over my head each morning; I could think of plenty of other things I needed to do, so it seemed like a waste of time.

While on my soulful journey, I implemented my new mindset when it came time for my morning dog walks. Instead of looking at doing them as a benefit solely for my pet, I decided to look at them as a special treat for me, too. On these morning walks, I found my inner voice, which propelled my mission to purpose. It's where I found inspiration for this book, and where I continue to find inspiration for future endeavors. It's where I can work on myself, talk through any conflicts I may be experiencing, and come up with resolutions. By choosing gratitude, I've made those dog walks a productive time that I wouldn't have otherwise.

"When I have this, then I will be happy." Does this sound familiar? We always think about gratitude like it's in the future: "If I could just get that raise, then I'd be able to afford the boat I've always wanted, and I would finally feel like I've made it." Living in a state of gratitude means having great appreciation for the current moment, because that's all we really have—the past is gone, and the future is yet to come. If we continuously talk about having things in the future that we don't currently have, we practice the scarcity mindset, focusing on what we lack.

Being mindful and staying in the present was extremely difficult when my children were young because many days were just utter chaos. I found myself trying to get everything done—laundry, cooking, cleaning—all while playing hide-and-go-seek and make-believe. Juggling multiple duties at once may initially make us feel productive and accomplished, but the more we multitask, the less present we are and the more stressed we feel. For example, when you're watching your child draw a picture, but are paying bills at the same time, you're not able to completely enjoy that moment with your little one or give dedicated time to an important duty, so you're left feeling overwhelmed. Instead, if you can, sit down with them and ask them why they chose that drawing. What does it mean to them? Why are they using those colors?

When you can take just five minutes to be fully present, you practice mindfulness, lowering your stress and improving your mood. You absorb all of life's gifts in that moment because you realize that that moment is gone in the blink of an eye. By living in the present, you embrace gratitude, and chances are, everyone around you is feeling its positive effects as well.

Practicing abundance also helps build resiliency and perseverance, the cornerstones to success. Individuals with an abundance mindset look at failure differently than those who look at life through a scarcity lens. They don't look at failing as the end but as the beginning—part of the journey to success. Abundance seekers show resilience when they get knocked down; when they lose, they see the opportunity to grow, learn from their mistakes, and get better and stronger. We only see the masterminds and geniuses *after* they fail, not while they're actively doing so; everyone struggles at some point. What matters is how we react to these failures and overcome them.

When I was in sales, the word "obstacle" always gave me the shivers—it sounded hard. Many may argue that "test" sounds equally challenging, if not harder, but hear me out—according to the Oxford Dictionary, an obstacle is "a thing that blocks one's way or prevents or *hinders* progress." On the other hand, a test is merely a measure of skill, knowledge, or aptitude for a certain thing. To boost our abundant state of mind, we must look at life's obstacles—and failures, even—as tests.

Henry Ford, J.K. Rowling, and Steve Jobs all experienced massive failures, resulting in bankruptcy, homelessness, and recurring unemployment. If they had allowed failure to stop them from writing or inventing, think about how they wouldn't have touched millions of lives—history would look a lot different. But instead, they kept pursuing.

In 2003, a UCLA graduate student named Jamie Link discovered "smart dust" after the silicone chip she had been working on was ground into tiny pieces the size of grains of sand. Today, smart dust is used in military operations, medical procedures, drug-making processes, and supply chain monitoring.

My cousin Katie is a brilliant entrepreneur who develops and sells tech companies to big corporations. She's even created an app! It's difficult to see how someone like her, who has experienced global success more than once, could understand what failure feels like.

Katie was preparing to sell her first company to American Express several years ago. Her team had put all their time, money, and resources into this one deal—if the deal went through, it would be life-changing for everyone, and it would place her on the map as one of the youngest tech entrepreneurs in the world. If it didn't go through, inevitably, the company would have to close its doors. The fate of her whole company resided in this one coveted meeting.

Unfortunately, American Express ended up backing out of the deal. Knowing the company was on the verge of going under and that she wouldn't be able to make payroll the following week, at the last minute, Katie hopped on a plane. She took the

Red Eye from London to New York, showed up unannounced at American Express headquarters, met with the president of the consumer group, and convinced her to go through with the deal.

Katie could have seen "no" as the end, would have been forced to close her company, left herself deeply in debt, and many unemployed. But she chose to look at the situation with an abundance mindset and find an alternate route. She saw it as the beginning, not the end.

Facing rejection only made her a better businesswoman and stronger entrepreneur. If she had used the scarcity mindset, she would have lost all the capital raised for that company and would have had to start her next start-up from scratch, setting her years behind. Her mindset was the only thing differentiating her from mega-success and utter failure. She has gone on to found four more companies since then.

So, let's reshape our thinking about obstacles and think of them as little tests from the Universe—you never know what might happen.

Practice Gratitude

You are abundant right now in this very moment. There is nothing you need that can make you abundant. It's that neediness that accentuates the lack mindset and blocks us from receiving the abundance that surrounds us. The Universe responds to our feelings, and it only knows the present. That's why it's super important not to put conditional restraints on gratitude, such as "I'll be grateful when..." If you're not feeling abundance, it's not because you don't have it; you just need help seeing it. That's where gratitude comes in. Holding gratitude forces you to be in the present, open your eyes to all you have, and increase your vibration to match your biggest desires.

Let's Journal

During my early abundance journey, I started a gratitude journal, which I continue to write in daily. I do this twice a day, morning and evening. I like to write in the morning because I begin my day with a positive outlook and a grateful heart before any curveballs are thrown my way. Then, I write down what I've learned throughout the day. This exercise takes me back through the day's events, helping me recall moments of happiness, inspiration, and wisdom. This practice also helps me end my day in a state of gratitude.

This is a real journal entry of mine to give you an idea of how to create yours. It doesn't have to be long:

2.10.23

Gratitude list:

- Happy, thriving children
- Dr.'s appointment so that I'm able to put my health first
- Continued inspiration to write my book

Inspiring thoughts:

- Learn something every day
- Remember my mission: to help people
- Be patient, everything will happen when it's supposed to, trust the process

What I've learned (evening)

- Be open to all opportunities!
- Never underestimate the importance of catching up with a friend
- There is ALWAYS another way

Paul Williams is a legendary songwriter who, at the height of his fame, struggled with an addiction to drugs and alcohol. After hitting rock bottom, he got sober and now helps others become better versions of themselves through a book he coauthored with screenwriter, director, and author Tracy Jackson, "Gratitude and Trust," which is comprised of six affirmations to help people discover their true happiness, potential, and purpose. When Oprah asked the two about the sixth affirmation, "Life and Service, Gratitude and Trust," Tracy explained, "If you have gratitude, then you don't have room for fear. Fear holds us back so much. Fear is what causes so much of our bad behavior and our poor choices. Gratitude can't live with fear, much like love can't live with fear. So, if you're grateful, you move to the place of love."

Oprah asked, "And what is trust?"

"Trust is God," Tracy replied.[6]

---

6 Super Soul Special: Oprah Winfrey: Grace and Gratitude, hosted by Oprah Winfrey, January 27, 2021.

Let's Meditate

I genuinely believe I would have been more successful and less stressed in my sales career if I had discovered this earlier, not to mention more in control of my reactions. For starters, I would have used meditation to problem-solve. Back then, my phone wouldn't ring because people were calling to tell me how happy they were with my product—no, they were calling because they needed my help.

It never failed. I would be in the middle of a task, and a customer would call with some crisis, catching me off guard. I would then absorb their panic and fly into damage control erratically and anti-productively. Suddenly, I spent my entire day trying to fix the problem, ignoring every other item on my to-do list, creating more stress as responsibilities piled up. Some problems were bigger than others, but at the end of the day, being the ultimate problem solver, I was spent, and I had nothing else left to give, personally or professionally.

Had I practiced mindfulness, I would have handled the problem completely differently, not reactively but with a solution-based mindset. This could have prevented the downward spiral of the day. We must expect the unexpected to happen—how we respond is all that matters. Visualizing your end goal reduces stress and gives you more confidence to tackle even the most difficult situations.

Depending on the situation, our relationship with abundance can originate from our past, so we must bring those feelings to the surface to set them free and create space for growth. We are all innately abundant; we all have everything we need within us, but it's tough not to get stuck in the external validation trap. When you focus on the lack in your life, I recommend an abundance meditation to bring you back to self. This will leave you feeling so much gratitude, so full of all the goodness that surrounds you, that the presence of scarcity will dissolve.

Close your eyes and take a deep, cleansing breath in, filling your lungs with fresh, energizing air, and then exhale slowly, releasing any tension or resistance. Allow yourself to relax into this moment, feeling your body grow calm and still. Begin to imagine yourself standing in a beautiful, sunlit garden—a place of infinite abundance. The air is warm and fragrant, and everywhere you look, there is growth and vitality: vibrant flowers blooming, trees heavy with fruit, and streams flowing with clear, sparkling water. This garden represents the boundless abundance available to you in all areas of your life.

As you walk through this lush garden, feel the earth's richness beneath your feet, grounding you in the present moment. With each step, repeat silently to yourself: "I am open to receive. Abundance flows to me effortlessly." Imagine golden streams of energy flowing from the Universe into your heart, filling you with a sense of gratitude and prosperity. This energy represents wealth, opportunities, love, and joy, flowing freely and infinitely into your life.

Now, visualize your life filled with abundance. Picture yourself achieving your goals, surrounded by supportive people, and experiencing all the resources and opportunities you need to thrive. Feel the emotions of this abundant life—joy, gratitude, confidence—as if it is already yours. Trust that the Universe is aligning to bring this vision into reality, and you are worthy of receiving it.

Take a moment to express gratitude for the abundance in your life, no matter how small. Each blessing is a seed that grows into more. As you breathe in, feel a deep connection to the infinite flow of abundance around and within you. When you are ready, take another deep breath, gently bring your awareness back to the present moment, and open your eyes, carrying the energy of abundance with you throughout your day.

If you are struggling with abundance, trying some inner child meditations specifically for abundance is also a good idea. As stated before, many of our blocks in adulthood stem from childhood "trauma" in some capacity. To cure this, we must focus on the parts needing healing. For example, suppose your family struggled financially when you were growing up. In that case, you could still hold onto those limiting beliefs surrounding money and feelings of unworthiness regarding abundance. You must learn how to release that burden that isn't yours any longer so that you can unlock the infinite supply of abundance and opportunity in your life.

Close your eyes and take a deep, calming breath in, allowing the air to fill your lungs, and exhale slowly, releasing any tension. Picture yourself standing in a bright, peaceful meadow, the sun warming your skin, and a gentle breeze carrying the scent of flowers. In this safe and nurturing space, you notice your inner child approaching you—a younger version of yourself, full of wonder and potential. They are holding a small basket, empty but ready to be filled. You kneel to their level, meeting their eyes with love and compassion, and say, "You are deserving of all the abundance this world has to offer." Together, you begin walking through the meadow, noticing the abundance: vibrant flowers, ripe fruits on the trees, streams flowing with crystal-clear water.

As you walk, encourage your inner child to collect symbols of abundance in their basket—flowers, coins, shining stars, or anything that feels meaningful. With each item they gather, affirm to them, "You are worthy. You are enough. The Universe provides for you endlessly." Notice their smile growing brighter as the basket fills, their confidence blooming with each step. When the basket is full, you sit together in the grass, and they hold it up to you, their eyes sparkling with gratitude and joy. You remind them, "This abundance is always here for you. You carry it within you, and it will never run out."

Now, imagine merging with your inner child, their joy and sense of worthiness flowing into your heart. Feel this energy radiating throughout your entire being—a deep knowing that abundance is your birthright. Take a deep breath, allowing this feeling to anchor into every cell of your body. When you're ready, gently return to the present moment, carrying your inner child's love, joy, and limitless potential. Open your eyes, feeling abundant and empowered.

Final Thoughts

When we focus on what we do have, we create more of what we want. We were all born with the innate feeling of abundance and love in its purest form. But to keep that sacred, we must combat the scarcity mindset (biological) and our superficial needs of acceptance (societal). We are brought into this world already with what we need to lead fulfilled, prosperous lives. It's our birthright to have all that we desire, and a universal law that states our dreams become reality when our energy aligns with our feelings. We create our realities based upon where we focus (or neglect) our love and attention, healing the wounds of our generational past to return to the most perfect and empowered version of ourselves.

Many of us mistake abundance for affluence, money, or success, when abundance is a feeling. It makes sense why I remember so fondly my happiest moments from childhood. They made me full of everything I could ever want or need in those moments, an endless supply of love, joy, and gratitude. Think of this as a filling mindset, like fuel in your car. We have to practice this so that the journey continues…just don't forget to slow down and check out the scenery.

CHAPTER 5

Inspired Action

NOT TRYING IS FAILING. – ANONYMOUS

It's scary when there are no promised outcomes. I think I've said to myself, "*What the hell are you doing*?" every day for three years at this point in my life. When I've overturned my career and driven my life into the uncharted waters of the unknown with no guarantees or promises on the horizon. I had no idea what the future would hold. Hell, I had no idea what tomorrow held—each day was like learning how to ride a bike again, but without someone telling you where to put your feet and hands.

Each day, I sat at my computer, taking turns staring at the screen and my phone. Should I reach out to friends and past colleagues to network more? Should I dive into the content creation world, learn how to create entertaining reels so I can go viral?

I had no idea what I was doing and suffered immense impostor syndrome on the reg. So fondly I remember the day when I was on a Zoom call with a sales consulting agency that pairs sales organizations with fractional executives—seasoned professionals who provide guidance and expertise to businesses. Now, let me first say that I researched this firm on LinkedIn and liked the culture it exemplified on the platform, so I applied to be one of the fractional executives. I thought it was a long shot, but they accepted my application and sent me a Zoom link. What I thought was an individual meet-and-greet with the CEO to get to know my background turned out to be a group of about 15 other fractional executives who had just signed on like me.

As the call started, the CEO explained that we were all going to introduce ourselves one by one and talk a little about our experience and our ICP. What's an ICP? Acronyms intimidate me. Maybe I'll just wait and see if anyone else asks. Also, *what am I doing?*

Of course, he says my name first, "Courtney Martin, why don't you start?"

"Hi, I'm Courtney. I live in the beautiful panhandle of Florida with my husband and two children. I was in medical sales for 16 years until I hit major burnout and quit. I now help organizations increase their revenue while decreasing turnover and burnout, utilizing a series of mindset practices. I give people the tools to reach their full potential in sales as well as in their personal lives so that they can enjoy sustainable success and personal fulfillment. And I'm sorry, but could you please tell me what an ICP is? I'm new to all of this."

"An ICP," he explains, "is your 'ideal client profile'".

Got it. No idea.

"My ideal client is any sales organization because I believe everyone could benefit from a mindset shift."

I took a deep breath, peeked at the screen of faces looking back at me, and tried to act cool. That wasn't too bad, right? The next person was called, "William, your turn."

"Hi, I'm William, and I am a fractional COO with experience as a 2x COO in scaling B2B SaaS and marketplace businesses from the seed stage through Series C. I've built and managed all business functions—GTM, Customer Success, BizOps, and Finance—and scaled the company 70x in four years. Previously, at Apple, I managed a $2B business and was consistently recognized in the top 5% of employees. My ICP are B2B SaaS businesses."

Never mind, mine was bad.

Every other person sounded just like William. I felt so incompetent and totally out of place. *What am I doing?* Also, how will I learn all these acronyms?

I suddenly caught myself longing for the days of predictability, the days when I could do my job with my eyes closed and get paid for it. Maybe I traded happiness for adequacy and self-assurance, but the latter seemed preferable right now.

The following week, I had a professional photoshoot scheduled. I had never done this before, but I knew if the internet was going to take me seriously, I needed to look like *I* took myself seriously. I was instantly struck with discomfort when I showed up at the studio. Still, after an outfit change, I found myself in front of the camera. The photographer started snapping pictures while instructing me to do all kinds of poses—every little and big girl's dream—but all I could think about was how incredibly out of place I was. What was I doing there? I was a nobody, having pictures made like I'm some superstar. I had the photographer fooled; I bet she thought I was a somebody.

Impostor syndrome is something I had never experienced before. Sure, I've had plenty of moments of insecurity, low self-esteem, and self-doubt, but this was something new. I felt like I was pretending to be someone I wasn't. (Like a poser, if you were a

'90s kid like me.) And as excruciating as it was to push through the acronym-laced Zoom calls, the awkward photoshoot, and the intimidating Instagram reels, I did all of it because I knew I had to. I didn't feel like myself. It didn't feel natural or good; it felt uncomfortable, and I didn't know what I was doing. Yet, I knew that to become the person I wanted to be and have the things I've never had before, I had to do things I've never done.

I learned how to control my thoughts and seek abundance, and I knew how to set and reach goals successfully. I fought hard to find my why and uncovered limiting beliefs from childhood along the way. I thought I was equipped with everything I needed to step into the life waiting for me. Wasn't that enough?

Nope. Now, I had to take inspired action.

This step was the hardest because it forced me to change and *align* my behavior with the most empowered version of myself. My self-sabotaging thoughts were at their loudest because they wanted to stop this change. Yes, this change was scary, unreliable, and uncomfortable—because it's supposed to be. Change is not easy, so many people never leave the daydreaming state. Changing and aligning behavior separates dreamers from doers, and finally, I became a doer.

After months of hard work dedicated to marketing myself and my course, I was asked to conduct a speaking engagement for the Pensacola Women's Alliance, whose mission is to empower professional and entrepreneurial women in the community through networking, mentoring, and serving. When a board of directors approached me about this opportunity, I was caught off guard and was about to answer, "No, I don't speak, I'm just a coach." I had never spoken in front of a large audience before and didn't think I was ready. But in the split second before answering, I heard a voice that said, "This is it. This is the moment you must take a leap to get you to where you want to go," and I said, "Yes."

I didn't have the skill to create a compelling speech then, so I immediately began working with a keynote speaking coach. I wanted to cultivate the ability to deliver intriguing and inspirational messages— to captivate their minds and sing to their hearts, not just to motivate. I spent all summer practicing in front of my dry erase board, talking to the imaginary crowd while visualizing the room with all eyes on me. I went over my presentation, on utilizing mindset practices, at least four to five times a day, trying to get through once without needing my notes. I wanted to be smooth; I wanted the words to roll off my tongue so effortlessly and polished.

After months of being coached, changing, editing, erasing, and then changing again, the day had come. I remember doing one last run through in front of my pretend audience before I left, wishing I could take them with me. I arrived at the Pensacola Country Club, where PWA meets, and felt confident walking into the room. I looked at all their inquiring faces and smiled, praying I wouldn't disappoint them. And for the first time in my life, I was handed a microphone.

My voice a little shaky, I began. Trying not to hear the echo of my own voice, I talked about my life as a corporate saleswoman, working mom, and spouse trying to navigate the day-to-day all while being completely exhausted and unfulfilled. I told the audience about my grandmother, how much she meant to me, and how her death killed a part of me but also awakened my soul. I spotted my mom in the crowd, and my eyes filled with tears as I told the story of Meme's last breaths—we shared the same hurt. But I knew I had to keep it together. I had about 25 minutes left, so I took a pause, a deep breath, and continued my presentation.

I surprised myself.

As I settled in, I felt like I was born to speak, going off script sometimes as I grew more comfortable in front of the crowd. I was shocked at how natural it felt, in my element and enjoying every second. Afterwards, one by one, women approached me to thank me for my presentation, telling me stories of their own triumphs and tragedies, asking for my business card, and inquiring about ways to work with me. I was so grateful to each and every one of them, so humbled by their kind words of affirmation.

My PWA presentation led me to three other speaking engagements, one in front of 325 women on a live Zoom call. The number was intimidating, but the fact that I couldn't see all their faces, especially their expressions, frightened me. How would I know if they were enjoying it? How would I determine if they were getting anything out of it or sleeping? Talking into my laptop, I focused on the fact that I could reach so many people across the country all at once. People I would never get the opportunity to connect with if not for this modality. I knew I had to pivot my thoughts from skeptical to confident.

I decided to give it my all. As I presented, I gave more energy than usual to keep the masses engaged and had to be intentional about asking questions in the chat section to confirm I wasn't on mute. After I finished, I saw people posting in the comments words like, "I love this!" and "This is the most compelling Zoom I've ever been on!" I had 15 people sign up for a call with me that night, and more in the following days.

Soon, I started getting clients, speaking more, and collaborating with other entrepreneurs to create bigger programs. People wanted to hear what I had to say, they wanted me to share my knowledge with them, and they wanted to know how to lead lives of success, empowerment, and fulfillment. I had no idea how my story and message would resonate with so many women needing to hear they could have it all, and not only that, they were *worthy* of having it all.

I was cooking dinner a few months later; my son was studying his spelling words at the kitchen island while I prepared chicken fajitas on a cold February night, when the thought suddenly dawned on me that every one of my visions had come true thus far. I stood there, spatula in hand, staring down at my sizzling pan, steam rising in my face, as I recalled my visualizations from two years prior. I saw myself presentencing to a crowd, coaching clients via early morning Zoom calls in my upstairs office, coffee in hand. I envisioned a growing team of collaborators, holding weekly meetings to brainstorm project plans, pipelines, and strategies—each beautiful vision had been brought to life. As I was so busy building a business—wondering if I was doing it right, anxiously anticipating where it would all lead to, what would become of my dreams—I never stopped to recognize I was my future self whom I fought so hard to become—the woman whom I've met multiple times in my mind, the one I go to for advice and guidance. I was her. This only strengthened my trust in the Universe, and my visions began to soar to new heights.

It was a funny feeling. I had grown so much, had come so far from the desperate days of my dying sales career, but at the same time, I knew this was only the beginning. The only way I can describe this feeling is hope, confidence, or optimism. Sure, you need all of those to secure any business venture, but what I have found unquestionably necessary to having a life of your dreams is *faith*—faith that your deepest desires are on their way to you, in fact, they're already yours. You have certain dreams because God put them there for you to discover. Author, publisher, and hypnotherapist specializing in past life regression, Dolores Cannon, explains that the Law of the Universe states that if you can see it, then it must happen. See it as already accomplished, and don't worry about the how. When we worry about the how, we interfere with all the many ways the Universe works to bring our manifestations to us, limiting the Universe, so we must surrender to faith.[7]

A great example of this is when I attended "HR Roundtable", an organization for human resource executives that meets monthly at the Pensacola Chamber of Commerce. At the time, I had zero clients, zilch, nada. It was very early in the morning, and I asked myself about ten times on my way, "Why am I doing this?" I knew I needed to network, but I wasn't clear on how an HR meeting was going to help me get business. As I entered the conference room, I introduced myself to the woman in charge, who introduced me to another woman who turned out to be the PWA board member—the woman single-handedly responsible for launching my speaking career.

This unexpected speaking opportunity became pivotal in my career, proving that stepping outside my comfort zone could lead to unimaginable growth. It reinforced the power of saying "yes" to new experiences, even when the path ahead wasn't entirely clear. By aligning my behavior with success, I began to experience challenges with greater ease, as I had already shown myself I could overcome them. I didn't understand until now that it's the taking action part where we truly learn, grow, and push our limits beyond the boundaries in our minds. Without acting on my dreams, I wouldn't have learned the new skills necessary for where I wanted my career to go. Without leaping into the scary unknown, I would have stayed right where I had been all my life: waiting for my genie to show up.

---

7 Dolores Cannon, Transformation Conference, Ozark Mountain Publishing, 2012.

With this newfound momentum, I focused on expanding my reach and impact. That's when I began exploring the world of paid advertising, searching for the right strategies to amplify my message and attract more clients.

After launching "*The Winning Mindset of Sales*," I began looking into paid ads on social media platforms to generate more exposure. After months of researching different companies that help content creators sell their courses, I landed on one I liked and trusted, Tom Wirth. Tom and his advisors teach their clients the fundamentals of creating your offer, nourishing relationships, and closing the deal. Their goal is to get you making six figures in a month…a tough feat, but proven doable. In one of the modules I watched, it listed "Character Traits of a Winner":

- Disciplined
- Relentless
- Self-Belief
- Extracts Value
- Ownership
- Confident
- Coachable
- Asks for help
- Takes Action

After going over these traits, Tom says, "There is a cost to growth, and it's paid upfront. What you exchange for growth is comfort." I loved that.[8]

---

8 "How To Scale To $100K/M [BLUEPRINT]," Module 3, Elite by Instant Clients, online course, Skool, https://www.skool.com/instantclientsai/classroom.

I wrote down this list and his quote and placed it on my desk so I could look at it during my daily work. As I read this over and over, I began to tie each one to my own practices, the ones I teach and write about in this book. For example, "Coachable", "Ownership," and "Asks for help" are under the growth mindset umbrella, where you learn how to take constructive criticism and work on your weaknesses to cultivate your skills. "Self-Belief" and "Confident" can't be acquired until you dispose of your limiting beliefs, and "Relentless" and "Extracts Value" come directly from your 'why'. The only things missing were the "Takes Action" and "Disciplined" parts, which are monumental pieces of the potential puzzle, and that is what this chapter is dedicated to.

Discipline is Alignment

Being disciplined isn't about restriction. It truly is just aligning with your authentic self so that you can operate to the fullest of your potential. And sometimes, it means saying, "no".

A lot of what we do, we don't *want* to do—anyone out there agree?—and there is a lot of what we *have* to do, so shouldn't we be more selective with what we want to do? For example, how often have you had an upcoming social engagement that you wanted to get out of but felt guilty saying no?

I hate to burst your bubble, but unless you're the keynote speaker at a corporate seminar, you won't be as missed as much as you think you will be. Sure, your friends will wish you were there and may feel a bit of your absence, but I promise you, not being present will not ruin anyone's evening. So, start saying no to the things you don't *want* to do—this will not only empower you and put you in charge of your life, but it will also provide you with more time to do things that align with your goals, propelling you toward them.

Saying 'no' more frequently also helps with living in the moment, a topic we covered in Chapter 3. Our lives have become so fast-paced, and we juggle so much now, you may often ask yourself, "For what?" I'm learning that living life isn't about the monumental moments; it's about your everyday life moments. Sure, the tropical trips to paradise come with fun-filled memories, but those are far and few between. What comprises most of our lives are the seemingly mundane, routine, and unexciting daily moments—these define most of our lives.

COVID was an extremely difficult and sad time across our country and around the world, but it forced us to slow down. We had to stop. Looking back, my family made many great memories, such as making games, going on nature walks, camping in the front yard, and doing science experiments in the kitchen. This wouldn't have happened if we weren't forced to halt work, sports, and social events. Although it was incredibly challenging to get through with a four and six-year-old, I can't help but think that if the world hadn't stopped, I wouldn't have been able to spend that time with them. I lived in the moment then more than I ever had before, because there were no other distractions. This is why I have the memories: because I was present.

If we're too busy day after day, we miss out on most of our lives. Let's learn how to stop, say no, and enjoy the everyday.

One evening, my husband and I were invited to a party that all our friends attended. It was right after the holidays, and we were tired of late nights and searching for another babysitter. We found ourselves stuck between wanting a break in social obligations and not wanting to hurt feelings, so we decided to send our regrets and stay in. That Saturday night, we played games as a family, my daughter taught me a new dance, and we woke up on Sunday feeling refreshed and productive to begin the week.

Had we gone out and not stuck with our intuitions, we wouldn't have made some new memories with our kids and probably wouldn't have felt as motivated on Sunday morning. And guess what? I only received one text message the following day saying we were missed—not even from the host!

This brings me to a topic that I believe is one of our most important and empowering decisions. When it comes to alignment, it's important to protect your energy, meaning be picky when it comes to who you spend your time with. To put it simply, people can act as pluses or minuses. The pluses are little addition signs in life, people who leave you feeling better about yourself, warm and happy. You know these friends or acquaintances—they just make you feel good around them.

The minuses are those who leave you feeling depleted. These are the ones that make you feel insufficient, unworthy, and just plain not good. These names probably come very easily to you (thank you, primal brain). Sometimes, you can't pinpoint why you're attracted to someone and loathe another. This is because your intuition is picking up on something your brain isn't, and that gut feeling is undefeated. Pay attention to how you feel when you're around certain people, and note your mood and energy afterwards so you can make solid judgment calls in the future. This is self-love.

Jim Rohn, an author and motivational speaker, famously coined the phrase: You are the average of the five people you spend the most time with.[9] Think about the people around you – are they driven? Are they kind? Do they bring out the best or the worst in you? Evaluate the qualities these close friends or family

---

9 Quote attributed to Jim Rohn, source unclear.

members possess and ask yourself if they align with the most empowered version of you.

During this phase of self-improvement, it's essential to surround yourself with people who will support, encourage, and inspire you. We consider others' opinions a lot more than we'd like to admit—remember, our subconscious is where our thoughts, emotions, and memories reside, and they influence our behavior. We want to be sure those we allow to be closest to us raise our self-worth and confidence, and that they want to see us prosper, succeed, and be happy. These cheerleaders will help get you back on track, giving you the momentum to keep going.

As you evolve into the person you want to be, you may see some of the people you used to regularly be around a little less frequently. There are multiple reasons for this: it may be a friendship that has been a burden for a while, but you didn't know how to get out of it, or it may be because you begin to see your values no longer align with this person. You may just grow apart from someone naturally, because you're changing for the better. That's okay, and it's actually a good thing—change and growth are the ultimate goals.

Try to find someone or a group of people who are going through the same thing you are. A couple of times a month, I would meet a friend who had just quit her job to live a more purposeful life for coffee. Our paths were merely identical, so we leaned on each other for motivation and encouragement. It can be lonely going through a life-changing event by yourself, and it makes it easier if you find others going through the same thing. They will also confirm that you aren't crazy, which is helpful.

This is a personal experience that everyone goes through at different times, or not at all. Try not to hold judgment or allow others' opinions to deter you. Look at it as a "test" from the Universe and keep going.

Let's Act

Every self-development practice in this book up until this point is internal, meaning no one really knows what you're going through or thinking. Healing, subconscious work, seeking your purpose—all of it is done in the privacy of your mind. These methods are comfortable and safe because they're done in the confines of your thoughts, where no one can judge or dismiss them. When you go to *act* on your passions, you become vulnerable to others' opinions and viewpoints. When you go to introduce the shiny new 'you' to the world, you lose that safety net and immediately fear rejection.

How many times have you gone to act on an idea, but the fear of failing made you give up? It happens to all of us, but the fact is, we usually have no evidence of something failing; we just allow our limiting beliefs to lead the way. When we allow these thoughts of scarcity to overpower the inspired parts of us, we remain stagnant, never following through to see our brilliant ideas flourish into tangible products or services.

Elisha Gray is a great example of this. Elisha developed an early telephone prototype but hesitated to file a patent right away. He feared it wouldn't be commercially successful, and in the delay, Alexander Graham Bell managed to secure the patent first, taking credit for the invention.

The same principle applies when pursuing our goals—waiting until we "feel ready" often means waiting forever. Just like Elisha Gray hesitated and lost his opportunity, we too risk letting our best ideas slip away if we allow fear to dictate our actions. The truth is that readiness is not a prerequisite for success; action creates the momentum needed to move forward. When we push past hesitation and take even the smallest step, we prove to ourselves that we are capable and that confidence fuels further action. This is why embracing discomfort and acting despite uncertainty is so powerful—it rewires our brains to embrace progress rather than fear it.

You can't spell *action* without *act*. We have always been taught to think and *then* act, but the opposite can be true as well. I take a bootcamp class, during which we go back and forth from the floor to the treadmill in seven- to ten-minute HIIT (high-intensity interval training) intervals. It's very challenging because the interval training accelerates your heart rate for maximum calorie burn. Each time we get back on the treadmill after a difficult strength-training session, even though all we want to do is walk and catch our breath, the instructor says, "Get into your jog, not because you're ready, but because you're *not* ready." By getting into our jogs *before* our brain tells us we're ready, our actions tell our brain that we are.

When I finally decided to launch my business, I had to increase my social media presence, and the first place I started was LinkedIn. I filled out my profile with my business name, description, and picture, feeling like a professional.

As I scrolled down to the next section, I saw a spot for "Experience", which included the name of the company you worked for, employment type, and title. I sat there staring at the word "title". At this stage, I hadn't yet developed my course. I hadn't even settled on exactly what my business would look like. All I had was a name and an LLC, Courtney Martin Mindset. But I knew what I *wanted* to be—an entrepreneur and business owner. And I knew that to become who I wanted to be so badly, I had to act like I already was that person. So, after what seemed like a stare off with my laptop for eternity, I gave my fingers a pep talk and eventually typed out, “Entrepreneur”. Looking at the letters, my posture straightened, knowing I had just taken a major step in my life. There was no looking back.

Let’s say your goal is to be in the top ten of your company. Start by visualizing what this looks like: a successful, career-focused salesperson probably wakes up early, gets a run in, and eats a nutritious breakfast. Maybe they even repeat positive affirmations for a few minutes or visualize a successful customer meeting. They don’t get sidetracked by small daily challenges but instead remain focused on their ultimate goal. They aren’t afraid to step out of their comfort zone, approach new customers, network, or gravitate toward new opportunities. To be a top performer, this means you exude the type of confidence people find it hard to say “no” to.

You know the saying “dress for the job you want, not the job you have”? It’s the same logic—if you want a promotion, you don’t show up to work in pajamas, right? You *look* the part because that may help get you the job or title you want, not the other way around.

Let's Journal

To align your behavior with your goals, do the inner work discussed in previous chapters, stay disciplined, or at least follow the 80/20 rule (because weekends aren’t for discipline).

Let’s start with how you begin each day—are you waking up late and hitting snooze ten times before jumping out of bed and racing around to make it into the office by 8:00? I love sleeping in as much as the next person, but when I wake up with the rest of the family, I'm just asking for more of a chaotic, unorganized morning than I wanted. Is this you, too? Or are you waking up 10 minutes early, practicing mindfulness while enjoying a cup of coffee? Taking a morning jog before easing into your morning routine? I love getting up just 30 minutes early so I can have the house to myself to pray, meditate, or take the dog on a walk, knocking out a chore and some mindful time all at once. I have experienced that doing this sets me up for a productive day. I *want* to get things done and have the motivation to do so. The day's tone is set during those few minutes of waking up, so do yourself a huge favor and create a morning ritual that promotes positivity, productivity, and peace. And on the days I'd love nothing more than to sleep in, I remind myself that I'm practicing self-love by giving myself a few minutes of 'me' time.

Mel Robbins is a podcast host, author, and motivational speaker who is well-known for her TEDx talk, "How to Stop Screwing Yourself Over." In it, she explains that to step outside of your comfort zone and into a more rewarding, fulfilled life, you must turn off your brain's autopilot. A rule she lives by is putting her phone in the bathroom each night, so that when the alarm goes off each morning, she must get out of bed to turn it off. Now, this serves two purposes: to make her physically get out of bed and to place herself in front of the bathroom mirror, where she gives herself a high five. She explains that when you give someone else a high five, you're saying, "Great job; you've got this," but we never talk to ourselves this way. By placing your hand on the mirror and giving yourself this accolade, you're starting your morning with self-love and putting into motion all the positive energy that will serve you throughout the day.[10]

Your nights can majorly impact your mornings, influencing the rest of your day's events: Are you getting enough sleep? Are you staying out too late, or perhaps drinking a few too many beverages, hurting your productivity and mood the following day? These are easy habits to work on because you will begin to make big changes, just by starting small.

I am my best self when I get seven to eight hours of sleep each night, eat a well-balanced diet, and move at least once a day. I'm like a weekend warrior—I try to be as disciplined as possible five days a week and leave a little room for treats and late(r) nights for the weekends. This is my balance. By Monday, I'm craving structure…and spinach.

I must have self-discipline during the week, and I can't fulfill my responsibilities if I'm tired or running on sugar and caffeine. When I don't feel productive, I go into a downward spiral of self-loathing, which causes unnecessary stress and more fatigue. Something I can prevent by putting my needs first.

Implementing healthy habits in your life will have a ripple effect—far-reaching benefits beyond just nutrition. These positive changes will result in a healthier mindset and emotional state, which in turn will permeate into every aspect of your life.

Take a moment and write down the things that hinder your motivation or goal attainment. Then, write down next to each one something you can do instead.

For example, instead of drinking alcohol, you could try drinking tea. Instead of scrolling through social media, you could write in your journal or read an inspirational book. And instead of sleeping in, you could go for a walk.

---

10 Mel Robbins, "How to Stop Screwing Yourself Over," TEDxSF, June 2011, https://www.ted.com/talks/mel_robbins_how_to_stop_screwing_yourself_over.

At the end of each day, I want you to acknowledge which actions helped you move closer to your goal and which ones slowed your progress. Sometimes we don't realize that some of our daily habits stand between us and who we want to become. Don't use this exercise as a way to punish yourself. Instead, use it to improve and become aware of how your actions make you feel. Then change those actions that are inhibiting your self-worth.

To live the life you desire, to become the most empowered version of yourself, you must also learn the art of self-forgiveness. Forgiveness is so freeing, and yet so difficult to do at times, especially when it comes to ourselves. We have all done things and acted in ways that we aren't proud of, and we continue to hold onto many of those feelings of anger, sadness, or guilt accompanying our missteps. But all that living in the past and holding onto resentments keeps us from manifesting our best selves.

Perspective plays a part in this because, like we've already said, our past experiences shape our mindsets. Suppose we continue to allow these past negative experiences to dictate our present lives. In that case, we will continue to live in the past and sabotage any potential for personal growth. By not forgiving ourselves, we allow our past mistakes to shape our future.

If you keep beating yourself up for things you said or did in the past, it's time to let them go and to begin the healing process. To set ourselves free from the anchors of our past, we must first acknowledge the things weighing most heavily on us.

Write down the past experiences causing you the most internal unhappiness—the ones you'd like to free yourself from. With each one you write down, I want you to practice powerful visualization by placing yourself back in that place, with the same people, even in the clothes you wore. Think about how you felt, how you reacted, and the words that were said. Allow yourself to be fully submerged in these memories, no matter how uncomfortable.

Now, repeat these sentences I took from Roxie Nafousi's *Manifest:*[11]

I was doing my best at the time.

There is always a valuable lesson to take from any and every experience.

I am not the same person I was then: I have since grown, evolved, and matured.

Look at each item you wrote and repeat those three sentences. Now, write down how you could have acted or responded differently.

Then, I want you to envision these regrets coming off the paper and evaporating into thin air. When you bring them to life, you're taking away their power over you; you are no longer allowing them to have a say in your thoughts, actions, and perspective moving forward.

---

11 Roxie Nafousi, Manifest (Chronicle Prism, 2022), 57.

Let's Meditate

Taking action toward your dreams begins with a single step—a choice to move forward despite uncertainty. Too often, we allow fear, doubt, or hesitation to hold us back, waiting for the "perfect" moment that never arrives. However, true progress comes not from waiting, but from doing. This meditation will guide you toward confidently embracing action, releasing self-doubt, and stepping fully into the life you are meant to create. With each breath, you will align with the version of yourself who takes bold, intentional steps toward success, knowing that every effort brings you closer to your goals. Let's begin.

Close your eyes and take a slow, deep breath in, feeling your chest expand with fresh energy and possibility. As you exhale, release any doubt, hesitation, or fear holding you back. With each breath, allow yourself to sink into a calm, confident place, knowing that you can turn your dreams into reality.

Now, visualize yourself standing at the beginning of your path. It stretches out before you, winding through unknown terrain, yet leading directly to the life you desire. You may not see every step ahead, but you know that movement is the key to unlocking new opportunities. Each action you take, no matter how small, is a stepping stone guiding you forward. Feel the excitement build within you as you take the first step, knowing that progress is created not by waiting, but by doing.

As you continue walking, notice how the path begins to shift, opening up in ways you couldn't have predicted. With every choice, every effort, you build momentum. Your confidence strengthens. The fear of failure fades, replaced by the understanding that each challenge is simply a lesson, each setback a redirection rather than a defeat.

Imagine yourself one year from now, having taken consistent action toward your goals. Feel the joy of accomplishment, the pride in your persistence. See the doors that have opened for you, the growth you have experienced, the transformation that has taken place. This future is not a distant dream—it is the result of what you do today.

Breathe deeply again, anchoring this vision into your reality. As you exhale, commit to yourself. Commit to action, to movement, to trusting the process. The time is now. You are ready. Take the first step, and the path will unfold before you.

Final Thoughts

Taking intentional action despite discomfort is the key to breaking free from the limitations of your primal brain and rewiring it for success. As you know by now, our brains are designed to favor safety and predictability, which is why change often triggers fear, self-doubt, and resistance. However, when you repeatedly push past these feelings and take action anyway, you weaken the old neural patterns that associate change with danger and strengthen the ones that associate it with growth and opportunity. Over time, what once felt terrifying becomes second nature. You develop resilience, problem-solving skills, and a mindset that sees challenges as stepping stones rather than obstacles. This shift propels you toward your goals and transforms you into someone who thrives on continuous improvement. The more you train your brain to embrace change, the more effortlessly you move toward success, making inspired action a natural part of your life.

Now is the time to be proactive and realize your dreams. You have to put your newfound knowledge into motion and trust that you will create the life you've always wanted by working through these mindset practices. The time to show up for yourself and take action is now. By doing so, you're telling yourself—and the world—that your self-worth is a priority. You are worthy and capable of great things, and to have something you've never had, you must do things you've never done.

Remember, our brains don't like being pushed outside their comfort zones, but this is the sweet spot—you're growing. By changing habits and behavior, you're strengthening your neural pathways and telling your brain you're already this new-and-improved being, capable of reaching your goals. By doing so before believing, you automatically adopt the new behaviors aligned with your ultimate goal.

This step was the hardest for me, and if it is for you, just keep going. Consistency and discipline will energize you as new ideas flourish and positivity flows. Your brain will create its own momentum because, thanks to your powerful visualizations, it's now wired differently. You have your roadmap and gas in your car—now, it's time to hit the accelerator.

Conclusion

I hope this book has shown you that you can change your situation, whatever it may be. It wasn't long ago that I was in a dark place in my career, with a toddler and baby on the way. I allowed the shortcomings at work to infiltrate my personal life, which I still regret. The work stress I brought home impacted how present I was as a wife and mother, ultimately creating an empire of guilt, frustration, and unfulfillment, which negatively affected my work. We are a lot to many in our lives—parents, spouses, employees, daughters, sons, friends, volunteers, and a whole lot more—but we can't successfully fulfill any of these roles if we aren't granting ourselves love, grace, and forgiveness.

My "self-actualization" journey, it turns out, was the beginning of my inner healing. I had to heal my past and the open wounds that needed love. Every scar from our past bears great opportunity for infinite potential, so explore the pain these scars symbolize and work with compassion on bringing them to the surface for their final voyage. We can see and feel our beauty, authenticity, and truth within that disembarkment.

The barriers that once held you back were never walls—only illusions, stories you had the power to rewrite all along. By choosing to release self-doubt, to see possibility where fear once stood, and to embrace a mindset of abundance, you have stepped into the limitless potential that has always been yours.

Hold onto your vision, nurture it with gratitude, and trust that the Universe always works in your favor. You become unstoppable when you align your thoughts, energy, and actions with purpose and passion. The life you dream of is not just a distant hope but a certainty, waiting for you to claim it.

Procrastination is the thief of motivation, so stop letting it hold you back from fulfilling your dreams and goals. You do have the time—it's all about how you prioritize what's important to you. Highly successful people say "no" more than "yes" because they know how to set clear boundaries. Remember: You can say no, so start saying it more often about things that detract from your accomplishments.

Don't get discouraged if you see relationships begin to change—that's a sign that you're aligning with your true values. Relationships you once thought healthy may start to fade because your intuition is heightened, and you may realize they are no longer serving you. The opposite holds true as well—you may find yourself being attracted to new groups of people based on their behaviors, interests, and qualities.

Don't put too much pressure on yourself to the point where you find this process a burden. That will only make it more challenging and less fun for you. This journey is supposed to be met with curiosity, excitement, and enjoyment, and when you see it as such, the answers will expose themselves to you automatically.

You'll know when you're moving in the right direction because you feel it first. You know you're making progress when you feel less anxious, more at peace with your life. Take this as a sign you're moving closer to your purpose. You'll suddenly let go of stresses, worries, and concerns about the future because you've just begun to *know* the life you've always wanted is well within reach.

Thank you for allowing me to be a part of your journey. And it *IS* a journey. You are meant to experience a thriving life, so don't waste another second merely surviving it. Invest in the self-work required for growth. You don't go to bed wishing for abs and then wake up with a six-pack—if it was that easy, everyone would be supermodels.

Self-work is required to change your reality, just as work is required for anything you seek to change. Change requires hard work, persistence, and absolutely the right mindset, and it's a continuous process. I still work on myself every single day because I know I'm worth it. I hope this book has helped inspire those qualities in you and that the ideas shared here will continue to facilitate your road to greatness.

Revisit those memories that have become frequent flyers—their presence serves far greater purpose than random echoes from your past. They could be your higher self-nudging you toward your soul's purpose, in the form of a bubbly second grader. Or they could be the source of unhealed wounds needing to be uncovered and released for self-elevation and empowerment.

Don't be so quick to brush these recollections aside. They could be the portal to a life you never thought imaginable.

Desire for our highest potential is not only a common thread that binds us but also the tapestry woven through our shared existence. Mankind has an innate need for an increase in food, shelter, and knowledge, just as tiny seeds seek an increase in water, sunlight, and *life*. Biologically speaking, we wouldn't be here without that desire for advancement. We want to get faster, better, smarter. We can't help but have this unquenched thirst for improvement, always, in all aspects of life, permeating our essence for fulfillment, abundance, our 'something more'. Each of us has a *more* dwelling within us waiting to be unearthed. Give yourself permission to find yours and follow it, not on foot but in heart.

Now, go forward with confidence. Live boldly. Dream expansively. Trust fully. Your journey is unfolding exactly as it should, and everything you desire is already coming your way.

I know you can do it. It's your job to know you can, too.

Don't wait for life to happen to you.

You are the artist, the creator—it's your story to write.

Photos

Bell Family beach cottage

Meme's Sunday supper table

Left to right: Jared, Harry, Courtney and Amelia Kate

www.ingramcontent.com/pod-product-compliance
Lightning Source LLC
LaVergne TN
LVHW010700110826
845149LV00014B/3175

* 9 7 8 1 9 6 4 6 8 6 7 9 0 *